How to Save Money On Almost Every-thing

Comments

You . . . offer sound advice on economical shopping and household management. . . . We all, rich or poor, need to stop food waste.

Dr. Jean Mayer,
consumer columnist
Professor of Nutrition
Harvard University,
School of Public Health

A practical guide for a consumer-oriented society gone crazy.

Dr. Arthur E. White
Eastern Regional Chairman,
National Institute for
Christian Financial
Planning

A most . . . informative book about making ends meet . . . while providing adequate nutrition.

The Honorable Lloyd Bentsen,
Senate Finance Committee
United States Senate

Neil Gallagher was born in New York and educated in Massachusetts and Rhode Island. He served in Northern Thailand as a Peace Corps teacher and medic in leper colonies during which service he received the Thai Foreign Service Award. In 1966 he was elected to Outstanding Young Men of America.

He has written twenty-five professional and popular articles, including articles for *Philosophy and Phenomenonological Research, The Journal of Psychology and Theology,* and *The Christian Science Monitor,* and two books, *How to Stop the Porno Plague* and *Don't Go Overseas Until You've Read This Book.*

He holds a Bachelor's Degree in History, an M.A. in Religion, and an M.A. in Philosophy. Following Ph.D. studies in a joint program of Philosophy and Psychiatry at the University of Cincinnati Graduate School and College of Medicine, he is focussing his efforts on writing.

How to Save Money On Almost Every-thing

Neil Gallagher

Bethany Fellowship INC.
MINNEAPOLIS, MINNESOTA 55438

Published by Bethany Fellowship, Inc.
6820 Auto Club Road, Minneapolis, Minnesota 55438

Printed in the United States of America

Library of Congress Cataloging in Publication Data

Gallagher, Neil, 1941-
    How to save money on almost everything.

    Includes bibliographical references.
    1. Consumer education. 2. Marketing (Home economics)
3. Cookery. I. Title.
TX335.G355   640.73   78-19113
ISBN 0-87123-234-0

Thank You

No husband
  . . . no heat
    . . . no lights
      . . . no food
In New England December.

And she sang and danced before thirteen-year-old and ten-year-old sons who forgot they were hungry.

Foreword

The author is calling for a change of life-style on the part of the American consumer. We can no longer buy now and question later. Neil asks us to consider why we shop and how we cook for best results. He shows his readers how, through thoughtful purchasing, one can save on common daily purchases. In an age of energy shortage, he requires that we know not only how to drive more economically but to be aware of how we can save even on auto repair and maintenance.

Since the great depression days Americans haven't been led to give much thought to how a dollar is spent. Now, if a family is to avoid going into debt beyond recovery, every member has to look long and seriously at how family income is spent. For too long Americans have bought the package without questioning the contents. The energy crunch, inflation, recession are forcing us to inspect the contents for quality, quantity, and nutritional value.

By pointing out the thoughtlessness and carelessness which an age of plenty fostered, Neil has done a great and necessary service to a generation of Americans in transition. We have come upon a detour on the road to prosperity. The way is bumpy, unfamiliar, and full of potholes. Circumstances within and without our control have brought us up short. The maddening pace has slowed. Now we are forced to think of the starving child in Bangladesh, the leper in Thailand. Their plight is not now so remote. The detour will be a curse to those who continue a thoughtless path and a blessing to those who hear the message that God is trying to impart.

—James R. Underwood, President
National Institute for
Christian Financial Planning

Lack of self-control is our No. 1 problem. For the individual, it takes the form of wasteful spending, leading to debt, gluttony, absenteeism, drunkenness, divorce, free sex, drug abuse, violence, and crime. For the city, state and nations, it comes as deficit spending and a "printing press mentality" whereby we print money to pay for our profligacy.

Pat Robertson, President
Christian Broadcasting
Network (in "Pat
Robertson's Perspective,"
April 1977)

Table of Contents

Chapter 1

The Rape of Hunger

I don't know why he was sick all the time. No one else's father was.

Coughing, wheezing, choking, in comas, in hospitals. When would he get well? When would we be a "normal" family? I guess never.

His TB put us on welfare. Taking him from his wool-sorting job—in a damp, dirty mill—it laid him in a Boston sanitorium.

Things never got better, only worse. And only to us—that's how it looked to a hungry thirteen-year-old clothed in Salvation Army discards, crouched in an icy corner room in December.

Suicide. Why not? At least I wouldn't have to look at those guys anymore.

Look at them: Charlie Grady, Eddie Wacker or Lennie Gaboury. They lived in matchbox tenements like we did. But the rest was different.

They had refrigerators. They had heat in the winter. They had paychecks coming in each week.

They never had lights and heat shut off. They never were evicted in the chill of winter. They never were denied food. (As many times as it happens, you never get used to having a glass of water for breakfast . . . and lunch . . . and supper.)

They didn't hear dishes, pitched at a drunken father, smash against kitchen walls. They didn't hear a mother wail and scream, watching beer destroy a sick man and money for beer seize food from the mouths of two sons.

And Grady and Wacker and Gaboury were never blasted out of bed by a pale mother wailing, "He's gone again. Come in here!" And we did.

Because of beer-drinking, eating poorly, and failing to take adequate insulin he, a diabetic, swooned again into a coma. Morning after morning, we poured orange juice and sugared water down his gurgling, resisting throat.

Why do I have to be the only kid in school who can't bring friends home? Why do I have to be the only kid without a dime to buy a waxed cup of ice cream in the cafeteria? Why do I have to be the only kid who can never buy a Coke on the way home?

Why can't we ever buy fresh milk? Why do we always have to drink that yellow, lumpy, and powdery stuff in dust-brown bags that welfare gives us? And why do we—my brother and I—have to be the only kids in the boy scout troop wearing patched street-clothes instead of crisp uniforms?

Because welfare doesn't give money for a dime's ice cream, or a Coke, or fresh milk, or a boy scout uniform.

When I was fifteen I watched him die in my mother's lap. She was sitting, he was propped up across her lap. Frantically she rubbed her hands up and down his back, back and forth across his caved-in chest, trying to revive him. His mustard-yellow face fell back; his cold, damp body hung across her arms. Propping him up again, she rained tears on his motionless body, looking like *Pietá*—Mary in agony over a limp, cold form.

He died quickly. Her fierce loyalty had kept him alive for many years. It was over. He was dead.

It was mid-January. A drafty, grease-smelling, third-floor tenement in South Providence was the stage of death.

His death had occurred during a rare happy period in their lives. Following three months of separation, they had come back to live together. They were determined to stop screaming and cursing. They were determined to be actively thoughtful.

He was not going to drink. He was going to take his medicine conscientiously.

They had been reunited only a few weeks. No drunken fights. No comas. He really had been taking care of himself. That Sunday afternoon they lay down for a quick nap. His self-injected insulin shot wasn't due for a couple of hours. No problem.

But they overslept. She woke up and found him swooning off in a coma. Orange juice. Sugared water. He coughed, gurgled and swallowed. It looked routine. We waited. No response. More orange juice, more sugared water. It wouldn't go down. It filled and overflowed his open mouth, like racing tap water overflowing a full glass. Streams of orange spilled over his blue-gray lips, cascading down his salt-and-pepper stubbled chin. Too late. The doctor later said his heart simply could stand no more comas.

Funeral and burial arrangements were dictated by others. (Poverty's lousy for handling death.) We had no choice. We had no money and no insurance. I didn't understand what it was all about.

Mother went back to work for $40 a week. We couldn't afford our wood-rotted tenement. I looked for full-time work, but she insisted I stay in school. I finished high school. Then she urged me to attend college if that was what I wanted. I found forty hours of work at night and earned a degree during the day.

After graduation I joined the Peace Corps and lived on survival wages. Nursing and teaching in leper colonies in Northern Thailand, I lived on $50 a month (made $75 and sent $25 home). I returned to the States and did a year's seminary work living on $35 a week.

After marriage and entrance to graduate school we, during a seven-year stretch, raised two toddlers, worked on two M.A.'s and a Ph.D., and lived on $62.34 a week.

We made it—thanks in part to welfare's lessons in living on crumbs. Score one for the poverty of welfare.

But the positive scoring stops there.

Poverty humiliates and rapes.

You feel you have to say "Yes, Sir" and shut up. You feel you have to apologize for everything you want. And your sense of weakness ignites resentment. You develop a slave mentality.

But you learn. You learn that the gloom of poverty becomes a prison only when you allow it. You learn that the tough break called "no money" doesn't mean you have to starve.

You learn that "no money" depresses, but it doesn't have to defeat. It teaches that impulsive buying is suicide. It teaches a fearful respect for money—one you remember long after you're off welfare.

You *can* buy cheaply and eat cheaply in America. I did. You'd better too before there's nothing left to buy, to eat, or to burn in gas tank or furnace.

People are multiplying faster than inflation. And energy and resources are melting faster than the green bills in our wallets.

Chapter 2

Boats, Bubble Bath and Barbecued Chips

Americans use money like toilet paper: snap it up and throw it away—mounds of it. We hate to admit it. We lie to ourselves. We tell ourselves we're thrifty, even stingy. We tell ourselves we're big bargain-hunters, tight-fisted, tough, and disciplined. We rationalize. We do not confess to ourselves that we spend too much. We buy armloads of stuff we don't need and then we make excuses.

In our heads we replay pipe dreams of what ruthless shoppers we are. We know, however, our daily shopping is not like our dreams. We get frustrated and angry. We hate ourselves.

We desperately want to discipline ourselves. But it's tough. Madison Avenue so planned it. They tease us and gouge us to buy what we don't need. Like jellyfish, we float on their waves of advertising.

They wiggle rainbow-sparkling gadgets before our eyes, shove spoonfuls of steaming food before our mouths, and wave open decanters of cologne under our noses. They preen our vanity. And we give in, which only increases our anger and frustration. It's depressing knowing you're a jellyfish. Financial Marketing Associates say that there are always pressures on us to buy things. Our wants are greater than our needs. And advertisers help exert this pressure. This leads to purchasing things we don't really need and to buying without comparing values and prices.[1]

We tire. We lose grip of willpower and billfold. "Tight spending and ruthless shopping" is impossible. We give up. Hey! Don't give up. We can make it. Honest. And we can have a good time—a better time, actually, because we'll be happier *controlling* money, rather than money controlling us.

We can know, *you* can know, the personal power of self-discipline—the feeling you get when you know you're *not* a slave to impulsive buying. That's relief, brother.

What you hold in your hand now is a war manual. If you use it, it'll bring hope, satisfaction, and relief. Set it beside your stove, breadboard, sewing machine, and workbench. It's supposed to get grease-stained and dog-eared with years of use. It's a manual for attack.

Madison Avenue, you see, has been wrenching our money from us for a long time. It's time to fight back. I'm telling how I fought back and how you can fight back.

Last year, while working on a doctorate, my family and I (again) lived below the poverty line. In a tenement-choked, speed-dizzy northern metropolis, we lived on a stipend of $62.34 weekly, of which nearly one-half went for rent alone. But, still, that was rich living compared to childhood days.

Not struggling, "pinched," or "socio-economically deprived," we were poor—plain poor. Evicted from tenement after tenement, off and on welfare, holed up in dirty, drafty and freezing tenements during New England winters, we shivered and starved. I shuffled to school without eating and moaned at lunch as aromas of molasses-coated baked beans, meat loaf wet with onions, and steaming-hot buttered rolls streamed up and down the basement cafeteria. Scratched plastic trays, smacking on laminated tabletops and hundreds of howling, yelling voices crushed into one happy roar. But I never felt part of it.

I watched them eat. Pretending I was reading (and therefore "too busy" to eat), I watched them shove into their mouths forkfuls of beans, steaming mounds of meat loaf, and fistfuls of potato chips. Sandwiches thick with tomato slices and bologna, lettuce leaves overhanging crusts, were grasped in two hands and pushed into attacking mouths. And I watched them tilt red-and-white, wet plastic cartons to thirsty lips and felt cold, creamy milk sliding down my throat. I wanted some.

And I wanted one, just one, butterscotch-brown, saw-edged, undercooked, peanut butter cookie. But I went back to class hungry. Then I shuffled home hungry, staring at greasy-gray city sidewalks smeared with blotches of gum and whiskey-bottle splinters strewn like beach sand everywhere. I remember having a headache, whining stomach, weak knees and going to bed.

Millions knew this feeling during the Depression years. But this wasn't during Depression years. No, this was during

America's post-war boom years—the late forties, fifties, and sixties when everyone seemed to be making it. Except us. We didn't have the simplest appliance and—sometimes—we didn't have food or shelter.

That's not quite the case today. Believe me, I count my blessings. Even on $62.34 a week for four, caught in an inflationary tornado, we did much better than I did as a kid. We made it.

And making it is tough these days.

Unless you've been adrift in the Pacific for several years or sequestered in a Himalayan cave, you know that America has been whacked by an inflationary tornado. Meat, sugar, land, gasoline, paper have shot higher and faster than a moon launch. And few Americans have received raises equal to inflationary prices.

In panic many Americans have seized moonlighting for the answer. It doesn't work.

Sidney Margoulis said:

> The effect moonlighting has on family life is one of its most serious considerations. Take the case of a . . . couple in their early 30's who have three small children. The husband has both a day and a night job, and the wife also works. Their total income is $625 a month. But living expenses and debt payments are over $700. He feels he must hold down two jobs to meet his family's needs. But he will not consider reducing expenses, budgeting, or even discussing how they can meet their expenses.[2]

We've tightened belts for the first time, for many of us. Many Americans, for the first time, have asked, "Can I afford this? Can I *really* afford this?" For the first time, as their billfolds have collapsed, many Americans have been smacked with a stony, cold fact: "There's *not* more where that came from." Money does not ooze endlessly from bottomless wells, not even for Americans.

For the first time many Americans have learned the little piece of doggerel, drilled into Depression families: Eat it up, wear it out, make it do, or do without.

That fact has shocked us. It's grieved us. It's wounded us.

More than one American has winced because he hates his newfound and forced responsibility of sorting luxury from necessity. A Houston housewife whined, "If the price of hamburger goes up, we'll have to sell our boat." The reality of inflation has, very quickly, matured many Americans. But it's been tough. It's been tough because, since World War II, we've *not* had a guns and butter economy. We've had a guns and butter and boats, and bubble bath and barbecued chips economy. We could afford all of them. Our public resources were endless. Our private supply of money was endless, that is, if not in the present, at least in the future.

Americans invented and lived this motto: "If you want it, buy it now." Borrow if you have to, but buy it. Buy, buy, buy, buy. Buying is power. The more one buys, the more one blazes with power.

The American assumption has been that we really can buy and own everything we want—if not with cash, then with credit card, loan, or layaway. And, since World War II, we *did buy* everything we wanted and stoked the inflationary inferno.

Since World War II, we collectively have refused to employ the common sense principle of *not buying inflated items.* (We won't die without beef or Coke. Honest!) If Americans collectively refused, for example, to patronize the sky-high prices of meat, sugar, beef or soda pop, their prices would *have to come down.* It is the same with other products.

But we grab what we want, hang the price. The American compulsion to buy is an addiction, the cause of which is simple. We are teased, gouged and programmed to buy. Professional, profit-obsessed czars know how to pull our hands to our billfolds, emptying them on impulse.

"It's a *war* between seller and buyer." That's what some say.

No, it's not. It's a slaughter, because it's pros vs. amateurs. They are disciplined in the art of selling. We're untrained in the art of buying. *Business Week* remarked that American business forces are bent on getting everyone to "borrow, spend, buy, waste, and want." *Newsweek* remarked that America is now the land where "never have so many owed so much to so many."

We buy greedily because they tell us we need goods to be happy. We buy greedily because they tell us there's more money where that came from. We buy greedily because buying life's necessities has been cunningly crafted to be a soothing morning out every day.

Market surveys document that, quite often, Americans shop *not because they have to*, but because they want a relaxing break. Sellers, capitalizing on this, build their stores to be relaxing lounges to continue to bait us. They know once we're in the mall, supermarket, drugstore, or drive-in store, we're hooked. We'll buy more than what we need. They know how to ignite our buying mood into a self-engorging spree. Sellers are not out to serve us. They're out to seduce us.

Shopping is a serious job, to be executed only with planned strategy. But they make it "fun." Forget your cares, toss credit to the wind, and use Master-Bank.

In collusion with the sellers ripping off the buyers are the ubiquitous, money-waving businessess: loan companies on front rows of shopping plazas, banks—in cute decor of castles or cabins, nestled in suburban streets—bottomless credit card accounts, Master Charge and Bank-Americard waved everywhere. We can't resist. We borrow money we can't afford, to buy things we don't need. We borrow thousands in unearned, "unowned" money in order to buy, buy, buy. If we can't get enough from one loan company or bank, we'll go to another. We'll always find one that'll let us borrow more. We may have to pay an enslaving 35% interest, instead of the outrageous 18% interest, but we'll be able to buy. And our addiction will be satisfied for a couple of weeks or months.

The rock song "Higher, Higher, Higher" dramatizes the

"Oh, we're not looking for anything in particular. We're just here to spend money." *

---

*Courtesy *The Real Paper*, Boston, October 8, 1975, p. 3.

American compulsion for buying. We're drugged. We're hooked on gratifying our impulses of appetite. Old pleasures and possessions bore us. We lust for new and higher pleasures. We "need" new kicks.

And so we go into debt. We lie—and sometimes steal—to get new luxuries. And they become a bore, a common necessity. So we seek newer luxuries for new kicks. And the newer luxuries eventually bore, degenerating to the level of common necessities. And we demand newer luxuries for new kicks, and on and on.

The uniquely American definitions of "luxury" and "necessity" are viewed by other peoples with shock, laughter, or bitter anger. We're richer than Solomon, and all the world knows it—but us. Even the poor in America are rich by world standards. Our "necessities" are *the world's luxuries,* and our luxuries, on their tally, are obscene waste.

While a Peace Corps volunteer teaching and nursing in leper colonies in Northern Thailand, I lived primitively—like the people. Primitive to me, an American, with no electricity, no plumbing, no cars.

But I really lived nicely. I ate adequately and kept warm on cold mountain nights. I had work to do, God to pray to, books to read, and people to talk to. It was a good life.

Upon returning to America, I saw it. Like opening a door to a dreamy vista of Snow White and Prince Charming's castle, I re-entered America. Like in a fairy tale, I felt as if I were surrounded by lemonade ponds and lollipop trees, marshmallow bushes and peppermint-stick fences. I saw that most things in America were not needed. Most of America was luxury.

The American standard of living, I discovered, was worse than being hooked on drugs. A drug addict knows he's hooked. And he knows that with locked room and a friend to help, he can withdraw in a week. He knows that, once kicking the habit, he can move to another part of America, escaping those who'd push a fix on him.

Americans don't know they're hooked. When suspecting a desired item or habit is a luxury, we swiftly rationalize and convert (in our heads) the luxury into a necessity. Should we ever admit the item or habit is a luxury and try to withdraw from it, we need more than a locked room and a friend to help. Because wherever we live in America we'll be attacked again and again by 1500 commercial messages a day!! From TV, car radio, billboard, direct mail, sky-writing, on-street, knock-on-your door handouts, newspapers, magazines, lawn signs, and phone calls, the pushers hustle with another luxury "fix."

Resistance is hard. Once you're been surrounded by every house-cleaning gadget, every kitchen and patio trinket, every mirror-polished, flute-carved, audio-visual toy, and every vacation accessory, it hurts and humiliates to live closer to the level of *necessity*, rather than luxury.

After engorging yourself with big cars, big houses, big meals, it sort of comes naturally (with a relentless push from advertising goons) to demand bigger cars, bigger houses, and bigger meals. We are seduced to believe that we "need" new and bigger goods (and more of them) and, not surprisingly, the collection of goodies eventually owns us, not vice versa.

A "Letter to the Editor" said a lot about American "necessities":

> The natives are restive again over the price of groceries, especially meat. Should it come down to it, I will sell my 36-foot cruiser, one of my sport cars and cut my summer European tour from 30 to 15 days, but I'm going to have my meat. If we poor people would quit trying to live like the rich folk, the price of steak wouldn't be a bother.

Rich folk? That's us. Whatever it is—steak or a chalet—if Americans want it, Americans buy it.

And whatever it is, we can make it bigger and better. We can make it smell better, taste better, feel better, look better—and sell better. To the comfortable, we pile on more comfort, to the convenient, more convenience, to the luxurious, more luxury.

Check this out: A refrigerator with ice-cube trays doesn't get it for us. It must have an ice-maker. But that's not enough. It must have a window dispenser dripping ice cubes. Still not enough. It must have an outer spigot for ice water.

Every year the big four car manufacturers knock nuts and bolts together inventing minutiae to tack and glue in new models, jacking their particular models one hair's width above a competitor's models. The trend began simply and reasonably, and then was blasted out of reason. Power brakes, power steering, power seats, power windows, automatic lights, stereo-sound speakers, tape decks, sun roof, movable steering wheel, velvet upholstery, tachometer, garage radar-buzzer. No matter how comfortable, how fully equipped, how convenient, or how complex, we can pile on more.

Whatever it is, Americans can make it fuller, faster, fancier, thicker, richer, cooler, quieter—and costlier.

American food—the most abundant and nutritious in the world—is not enough. We want it instant—instant soups, coffees, juices, teas, desserts, TV dinners and pre-packaged skillet meals, and make it snappy.

If you can't package it for snappy preparation, sell it at a nearby drive-in or deli or chicken/burger/taco place so we can zip it out in ninety seconds. I don't care how much it is; just how much time will it take?

Americans supplement meals with tons of snacks, able to add a ton to an elephant: potato chips, pretzels, canned dip, frozen dip, make your own dip, bottled dip, ruffled potato chips, wavy potato chips, barbecued chips, onion chips, hickory-smoke chips in small, medium, average, twinpack, one-pound sacks, one-gallon cans and six-sack lunch size sacks. Fritos, doritos, burritos, tortillas, fried crunchy pork skins, bugles, twistees, party mix, whizzies, dizzies and frizzies. Crackers, cookies, cakes, chocolates. Wheat thins, bacon thins, garlic thins, cheese thins, sesame thins. (Who stays thin on all this?)

Pretzels, pizza, egg rolls, pralines, ice cream, cold cuts, cheese cuts—and Coke, lots of Coke.

It's a fight to stay either thin or thrifty when so many goodies grab dough from our pockets. They hit us at the beginning of the day with pre-packaged cereal. What an array of cereals they jam on supermarket shelves! It's a jungle taking one wall of each supermarket and grabbing kids' eyes and *our* money with krispies, koolies, sweeties, wheaties, shreddies, fruitees and charmies. You need the austerity of a hermit, the will of a mule, and the side blinders of a plow-horse to resist.

The cereal seduction ought to teach us this: the men who invent, package, display and sell *all* American food products are—listen!—out to get us. And, if necessary, they'll seduce our kids to get to us. It's war. And we're outnumbered. They'll give us an offer we can't resist. They always do and they always win.

One of the most cunning seducers, by the way, is television:

> . . . it has to be recognized that the shaping of American food habits is not being done by nutrition professionals but by food manufacturers. Sales and profits rather than sound nutrition are their goals. Television is the great food education of this country. A moderate TV-watching child sees about 5,000 food commercials a year: most of them about sugar-coated cereals; candy; gum; soft drink, and snack foods.[3]

The list of other "necessities" (former luxuries), sucking cash from our pockets to their vaults, marches on: cologne, after shave, before shave, talcum powder, scented spray, perfume, sachet, bubble bath, mascara, foundation cream, lip icer, hair spray, hair conditioner, hair rinse, hair color, hair dye, hair streaker, hair froster, hair remover, hair-put on, false eyelashes, eyebrow pencil, mouthwash, fragrant toothpaste, breath mints, breath gum.

Get this: if we wear it, eat it, live in it or drive it, some American manufacturer will give it more size, shine, smell and a big fat price tag. And Madison Avenue will goad us to buy it. Because we need it, of course.

The wonder is that our rate of inflation is so small!

How does a buyer win in this war? That's what this book is about.

For openers, know *why* you shop. Know *how* you shop. Know *why* you cook. Know *how* you cook. Know how to save money on two hundred common purchases from coffee to cars, from mattresses to meat.

Shopping. Get this in your head. I'll say it again: Americans rarely shop for the sole purpose of buying necessities. We shop largely because it's relaxing.

We like the rainbow colors of packaged foods, the dulcet tempo of the supermarket's stereo-music overhead and the ballroom-glossy floors. Shopping relaxes and entertains. We're fascinated by the glamorous gadgets and goodies neatly stacked. And we're bewitched with our feeling of power when we buy a pretty goody and clutch it to ourselves.

Know *why* you shop. Is it to accomplish the mundane chore of buying necessities or is it to be soothed and entertained? Examine your shopping mood: if it's more of the latter than the former, watch out! Your money's going in directions you're unconscious of. You're spending too much for things you don't need. You're spending time (and money) in places you don't need to be. You're grabbing luxuries. You're living impulsively and wastefully.

The following survey figures describe most of us. When Americans enter a store, they buy at least *TWO* items impulsively, *which, before entering the store, they had not planned to buy!*

Discipline yourself. Concentrate while shopping. Give yourself a time and dollar limit. Map a plan *BEFORE* you enter a store.

Cooking. Americans rarely cook simply for the required task of putting necessities on the table. Too often, we cook with a lust for novelty, variety and entertainment. We're obsessed with engorging diners (family or guests) and titillating their palates. (I'm not against good food; I'm against the abuse of it.)

Because of custom and culture Americans eat three meals a day. But our timeclock for our stomachs has been determined not by biological need, but cultural habits. Many, many people actually function better on two—or even one meal—a day. But, in America, we continue with the expense (and added fat) of three a day—because it's habit.

That's really what this book is about: habits. Learning what our spending and eating habits are and controlling them.

Chapter three gives two hundred maneuvers for saving money when buying and preparing food.

Chapter four gives low cost recipes. They're easy to prepare and tasty. Not luxurious, they're filling, cheap, and good for you.

Chapter five provides over a hundred attack maneuvers for saving money on nonfood items, including self-repair tips.

Chapter 3

Respecting Food, Defending Dollars

Lunch time.

Walk into any restaurant or cafeteria in America. Watch Americans eat.

Walk between their tables. Watch them pick and toy with hills of delicious deep-green peas, chunky cubes of gravy-soaked beef and saucers of fresh lettuce and glistening tomato wedges.

Fold your arms and lean against the wall abreast the black-rubber, wide tongue pulling in "empty" trays.

Heaps of food spill over plates as trays whack and clatter feeding down the long black tongue. Left-over everything overflows and streams down the sides of barrel-size GI cans, like lava erupting from a volcano, streaking down its grooved sides. Chunks of rolls, C-shaped teeth marks cut in the white inner edges, chicken legs with two bites ripped out, cubes of red and green jello bouncing in full bowls, half-mounds of creamy-white mashed potatoes, clumps of meat loaf dotted with green peppers, whole baked potatoes, peas 'n carrots untouched, half-glasses of milk thrown away.

Listen to the diners: students, businessmen, truckers, secretaries, congressmen, old ladies; white, black yellow, brown or red. "Same meat loaf today." "Bread looks day old." "Potatoes aren't hot." "Salad is soggy." "Gravy is flat." "Chicken is dry." "Jello again?!" "Peas are cold." On and on they groan, impressing companions with their discerning, picky tastes. They punch out soft centers of bread discarding the crusts, stab a fork indignantly into lukewarm potatoes, and pick aimlessly at a meat dish offered two days in a row. (Horrors!) The groaning convinces companions, you see, that they are food afficionados—discerning, tough, and regal.

All it shows is that they're rude, spoiled and overfed. (It also shows their pea-size egos; people big on criticizing are little on self-esteem.)

God forgive us.

Nutritionists say that the underfed multi-millions of Asia and Africa could eat on America's leftovers alone! As a Peace Corps Volunteer working in leper colonies in Thailand, I saw many of those underfed. In a Northwestern Thai village, roamed by scavenger dogs and baking under a ruthless sun, I saw a nine-year-old hunger skeleton: toothpick-thin arms and legs, no cushion of fat for his curved parallel ribs pressing against tightly stretched skin, a soccer-ball-size belly bloated with parasitic worms and a stumbling, head-drooped, chin-in-chest walk. His brothers and sisters were also skeletons.

Nutritionists say that the ten million poor in America could eat on the leftovers from the remaining 211 million. I believe them because, as a boy in a dying and depressing mill-town, I routed through cafeterias heaps of leftovers to find additional food. Food discarded by rich and fat fellow Americans.

Waste. Obscene waste. Americans not only tolerate it but applaud it.

How many countries promote pie throwing? How many countries stage pie-eating, hamburger-eating and watermelon-eating contests? How many countries regularly use healthy life-giving food merely for *decoration*? How many use parsley fingers for plate trim (and then throw away the parsley), lettuce leaves for jello-plate decor (and then throw away the lettuce), and tomato, orange or apple slices to build a fringe around hills of salad, potatoes, and meat (and then throw the fringe away)?

We insult food. We disrespect it. I don't know why God hasn't grabbed it from us long ago.

Food for Americans is not for survival, but pleasure. Food for Americans is for fun, not functional necessity. And the manufacturers and sellers exploit our frivolous mood.

The average supermarket fills its shelves with 10,000 items. *10,000!* We don't need that many choices to get the food we need to survive. Why that many? Because producers and sellers want us to embrace food as something more—much more—than a survival commodity.

They believe that if they crowd their shelves with sweet and pretty (albeit unnecessary) goodies, appealing to our vanity, greed, and lust, we'll buy them. They're banking on that. And they usually win.

They're *not* out to serve us. They're out to seduce us. They goad us to buy food and nonfood items which we emphatically don't need.

Tom Hall said it exactly right:

> If they really wanted the ultimate in good nutrition and price, then the food industry would devise some cheap, effort-less, and excellent nutrient like dog food. People would just reach into a paper sack and grab a handful and eat it. Nobody would be fat or have high blood pressure. Kitchens would become closets. Supermarkets would become filling stations. The average middle class American would be 10% richer, having saved most of the 15.7% of his income that he now spends on food. And he would have two hours more each day to do what he likes, having reduced his mealtimes to a grab and a swallow.[4]

To market their superfluous and inflated items, supermarkets construct glossy-tiled, stereophonic traps. Once we're in the trap, we are hooked for more than we need.

We'll continue being hooked until we practice *defensive* spending. And until we smack ourselves in the face with the shocking, icy waters of self-discipline.

The need for self-discipline becomes alarmingly obvious as we daily notice our buying power shrink. We actually have fewer purchase-power dollars now than we did ten, twenty, or thirty years ago.

"No, I don't. I've gotten raises!" you say.

So what?

In the past ten years, the cost of food has risen higher and faster than most wages. You may have more cash in hand, but it buys *less* than it did years ago.

In 1944, say, you earned $8,000 (a comfortable salary then). Bread in 1944 cost 9¢ a loaf. Today you earn $16,000. Your salary has doubled. Bread costs 50¢ a loaf. You got a 100% raise; bread rose 400%.

In 1944, one pound of coffee was 30¢; today it is $2.61. Your salary rose 100%; coffee rose 400%. In 1944, one pound of round steak was 45¢; today it is $1.98. Your salary rose 100%; steak rose 400%.

If you were making $8,000 in 1944, you'd have to be making $32,000 today just to retain the same purchasing power you had in 1944. Did your salary really increase four times since 1944? Or three times since 1955? Or double since 1965?

The United States Bureau of Labor statistics tells a grim story of a shrinking dollar.

How Your Dollar Has Shrunk[5]
(from 1944-1976)
U.S. Bureau of Labor Statistics, Consumer Division

Year	Round Steak 1 lb.	Sugar 5 lbs.	Bread Loaf	Coffee 1 lb.	Eggs 1 dz.	Milk Half Gallon	Lettuce Head	Butter 1 lb.	Stamp 1st Class Mail	Gasoline 1 gallon
1944	$ .45	$ .34	$ .09	$ .30	$ .64	$ .29	$ .12	$ .50	$ .03	$ .21
1954	.92	.52	.17	1.10	.60	.45	.19	.72	.03	.29
1964	1.07	.59	.21	.82	.57	.48	.25	.76	.05	.30
1976	1.78	2.28	.36	1.80	.84	.78	.43	1.10	.13	.63

According to the Bureau's *percentage* of increases, prices by 1980 will approximately be:

1980	$3.40	$4.29	$ .69	$3.61	$1.55	$1.51	$ .79	$2.19	$ .25	$1.19

That's not too cheerful.

You brighten the picture—and defend yourself against financial annihilation—by daily employing a shopping/cooking strategy glued to self-discipline and tough-minded planning.

Each time you shop, burn this in the center of your brain (again): the store is *not* there to serve you but seduce you. It's there to grab your vanishing dollars. It's there to attack.

Actually, it's more than attack. It's a massacre. It's the professionals vs. the amateurs, the greedy vs. the trusting, the war-horses vs. the tenderfeet. Either you shop defensively or you'll be slaughtered.

The store is physically plotted to attack. As you enter, you flow along the produce aisle. They engineered it that way. You just entered, you see, and you're glad to be out of the cold (or hot). You're relaxed and refreshed. They promptly push shiny-wet fruits and vegetables—with high mark-up—before you. They're out for your money from the start. They promptly grab your money by putting "sale" tables of snacks, sweets, and other luxuries in the middle of the entrance aisle. Your relaxed mood nudges you to grab a snack.

You flow down the produce aisle and to what do you come? Meat. You wheel your basket across the store and flow down the dairy aisle and to what do you come? Meat. You wheel to the middle of the store and flow down the sugar 'n flour aisle and to what do you come? Meat. They plot the store's aisles to force every shopper to constantly look at thick slices of glistening-red (and high mark-up) meat. On nearly every shopping trip, your eyes hit meat at least twice and maybe as many as twenty times.

On displays of high mark-up items, phosphorescent-pink signs flash: COMPARE! UNBELIEVABLE SAVINGS! WHY PAY MORE! The screaming messages attract as much as they mislead. (More of on how to read "sale" signs later.) But, knowing you *have to buy* sugar, flour and other staples, they don't tack phosphorescent-pink signs on them, nor do they pack them in orange and red boxes and pile them high on you-have-to-bump-into-it display tables. That is why sugar, for example, is in a plain yellow bag on the bottom shelf. You have to hunt for it until you find it. Not so with the high mark-ups.

After they've wooed you at cool produce, teased you with several offers of meat, grabbed you with psychedelic, eye-level signs, and bumped into you at aisle-choked display tables, they're out for the final rip-off at check-out counters. You're tired and hungry, so they herd you beside tables spilling with goodies. Candy, cookies, peanuts, soda, potato chips and fritos surround the check-out counters. They're so easy to reach, *especially for kids.* They look so good, especially since you're tired and hungry. Persistent, cranky kids whine for "just one." You cave in—like you've been caving in throughout the store.

Later that week, you stare at your checkbook nudging zero and look with horror into a billfold with three dollars lined up— and it's two weeks before you're paid again. You're ashamed, angry and confused. You vow that the store will never suck cash from you again for junk food and luxury gadgets. Keeping those silent vows is tough, but it can be done. That's what this chapter is about.

What to Do Before Entering a Store
(actually, before leaving the house)

Don't enter at all. That's right. Shop as little as possible. The less you're in a store, the less chance they have to grab your money. Shop once a month. Drink powdered milk and pack freezer with loaves of bread, protecting yourself from "picking up milk and bread" every other day.

Make shopping and cooking a business. Map details, plot strategy, analyze results.

Lois McBride says:

> Sit down one afternoon and plan all your menus— breakfasts, lunches, dinners and snacks—to take you through to your next shopping day. Then make up your grocery list, checking your cupboards as you go to be sure you will have all the ingredients you will need. If this seems like a chore, think of it as being a salaried job and make it more interesting by pretending you live in the Arctic and will all die horribly of starvation if you make a mistake.[6]

Set up a budget of how much you'll spend for food. *Spend only that.* If you run out, eat oatmeal or beans until you get paid again. But *spend no more than you've budgeted.*

Shop in a supermarket rather than a quick-stop, drive-in store. (You easily avoid the quick-stops by stocking up on milk and bread.) In quick-stops, you lose 5¢ to 19¢ on *each* purchase, as the chart shows.*

Product

Type of Store	Instant Coffee 2 oz.	Reg. Coffee 1 lb.	Loaf Bread 1 lb. 2 ozs.	Peanut Butter 12 ozs.	Can of Spam	Corn Flakes 12 oz.	Tomato Sauce 8 ozs.	Flour 5 lbs.	Toilet Paper 4 rolls
Super-Market	$1.46	3.20	.49	.83	1.13	.56	.25	1.09	4/$.97
Quick-Stop Store	1.61	4.69	.58	.99	1.69	.89	.38	1.19	4/1.29

(Price comparisons made on same brands, same locality, same time.)

If you have a choice between two supermarkets and one offers trading stamps, check its prices *very* carefully to make sure you're not wasting money on high mark-up items just to get a few stamps.

Examine newspaper ads and stores' poster ads. Phrases such

---

*Exceptions are dairy outlet stores selling milk, eggs and ice cream at lower-than-supermarket prices. However, the customers drawn in *then* buy additional items at higher-than-supermarket prices. A gallon jug of milk, for example, may sell in supermarket for $1.50, in dairy outlet quick-stop store for $1.42. But you pay dearly for other items. See chart.

as "Compare!" "Why Pay More?" "Look!" "Special," etc., do *not* mean the item is on sale. "Compare" (to what?), "Why Pay More?" (more than what?), "Look" (OK, I looked, so what?), "Special" (but I don't *need* it, regardless of how "special" the price is).

Hunt through magazines and newspapers for coupons. Keep all direct mail coupons and use coupons only on *necessary* items. If you buy a 95¢ *luxury* food, reduced to 75¢ by a 20¢ coupon, you've still wasted 75¢.

When a store advertises a sale or coupon redemption, call first to be sure they provide rain checks. In other words, if you shop for the sale item or coupon item and it is gone, a reputable store will allow you to pick up that same item later at the sale or coupon price. You protect yourself from bait-and-switch tactics of unreputable stores by confirming—by phone—the store's willingness to provide rain checks.

Before leaving the house, check with the local home extension agent or State Department of Agriculture to ask what foods are in season (and, therefore, cheaper). Check newspapers for surrounding farms offering "come-pick-your-own" sales.

Organize a floor plan for your shopping. (That's one advantage, incidentally, of shopping at the same place.) You'll get around the store faster and out of it cheaper with a floor plan.

Take with you a pocket calculator or pen and pad and total as you shop. Keep an eye on the register as purchases are rung up. If final total does not square with yours, find out why (Both stores and clerks can make errors.)

Shop with a buddy. You and the buddy restrain each other from buying impulsively.

Don't take your mate or kids with you. They have a tendency to say, "Why don't we get one of these?" "Let's try this!" "Aw, Dadee (or, Momee), just one!" One person, soft on impulsive buying, is a budget threat. *Four* is a disaster.

Don't leave the house to shop when tired, hungry or depressed. You're a perfect set-up for appetizing goodies!

And don't enter a store to "kill time." You'll end up killing cash. Don't enter a store "to take the kids for a walk on a rainy day." Your cash (and patience) will vanish.

Furthermore, don't be fooled by those press reports of "lower food prices across the nation," tempting shoppers to lower their guard. When this report was given, the press was fooled. A consumer action panel discovered the real reason behind the "lower food prices." Here's what happened.

Food prices, say, at 89¢ were reduced to 85¢ and the food's container kept the same dimensions. The 89¢ item had been packed in a 11" x 5" x 1" box, and the 85¢ item was packed in exactly the same 11" x 5" x 1" box.

The Consumer Action Panel discovered, however, that while the size of the box remained the same, its *weight* changed. The original package, weighing 16 ozs. at 89¢ (about 5½¢ per oz.) was actually reduced in weight to *13.5 ozs.*, costing 85¢. It appeared to many shoppers, including the press, that they were paying less for the same amount of food.

The Consumer Action Panel discovered that with the decrease in weight in the same size boxes, the per unit cost actually *increased*! For example, 16 ozs. of food at 89¢ costs 5½¢ per oz.; 13.5 ozs. of food at 85¢ (deceptively packed in same size box as the 16-oz. size) costs nearly 6¢ per oz. Yet the press reports headlined their articles: TWO SUPERMARKET CHAINS TRIM RETAIL PRICE.

They did *not*, unfortunately, decrease their prices. They actually increased them, and a lot of shoppers—including the press—were taken for a ride.

What to Do When You Enter the Trap
(Finding the Basic Four)

The first thing you must do is to find the basic four products and buy them first. These include the following:

Vegetable-Fruit Group

Items in this group are necessary as sources of Vitamin C and A. Vitamin C sources are: grapefruit or grapefruit juice, orange or orange juice, cantaloupe, fresh strawberries, broccoli, green pepper and sweet red pepper. Vitamin A sources are dark-green and deep-yellow vegetables, apricots, broccoli, cantaloupe, carrots, kale, pumpkin, spinach, sweet potatoes, turnip greens and other dark-green leaves.

Milk Group

This group includes milk (whole, evaporated, skim, dry,

buttermilk); cheese (cottage, cream, cheddar-type); ice cream and butter or margarine.

Meat Group

Beef, veal, lamb, pork, liver, heart, and kidney as well as poultry and eggs, fish and shellfish, comprise this category. Alternates may be dry beans, dry peas, lentils, nuts, peanuts, and peanut butter.

Bread-Cereal Group

Look for bread and cereals which are whole grain or enriched (check label to be sure). These include cooked cereals, cornmeal, crackers, flour, grits, macaroni, spaghetti, noodles, rice, and rolled oats.

The United States Department of Agriculture describes the benefits and uses of each food group.[7]

Vegetable-Fruit Group
(providing Vitamins C and A)

Contribution to diet: Vitamin C is needed for healthy gums and body tissue. Vitamin A is needed for growth, normal vision, and healthy condition of skin and other body surfaces.

Amounts recommended: Four or more servings every day: One serving of a good source of Vitamin C or two servings of a fair source.

One serving, at least every other day, of a good source of Vitamin A. If the food chosen for Vitamin C is also a good source of Vitamin A, the additional serving of a Vitamin A food may be omitted.

The remaining one to three or more servings may be of any vegetable or fruit, including those that are valuable for Vitamin C and Vitamin A.

Count as one serving one-half cup of vegetable or fruit; or a portion as ordinarily served, such as one medium apple, banana, orange, or potato, half a medium grapefruit or cantaloupe, or the juice of one lemon.

Milk Group

Contribution to diet: Milk, the leading source of calcium, is needed for bones and teeth and also provides high-quality protein, riboflavin, Vitamin A, and many other nutrients.

Amounts recommended: Some milk every day for everyone. Recommended amounts are given below in terms of whole fluid milk:

	(8-oz. cups)
Children under 9	2 to 3
Children 9 to 12	3 or more
Teenagers	4 or more
Adults	2 or more
Pregnant women	3 or more
Nursing mothers	4 or more

Part or all of the milk may be fluid skim milk, buttermilk, evaporated milk, or dry milk.

Cheese and ice cream may replace part of the milk. The amount of either that it will take to replace a given amount of milk is figured on the basis of calcium content. Common portions of various kinds of cheese and ice cream and their milk equivalents in calcium are:

1-inch cube cheddar-type cheeses = ½ cup milk
½ cup cottage cheese = ⅓ cup milk
2 tablespoons cream cheese = 1 tablespoon milk
½ cup ice cream = ¼ cup milk

Meat Group

Contribution to diet: Meat foods are needed for their protein, necessary for growth and repair of body tissues—muscles, organs, blood, skin, and hair. These foods also provide iron, thiamine, riboflavin, and niacin.

Amounts recommended: Choose two or more servings every day. Count as a serving two to three ounces of lean cooked meats, poultry, or fish—all without bone; two eggs; one cup cooked dry beans, dry peas, or lentils; 4 tablespoons peanut butter.

Bread-Cereal Group

Contribution to diet: Foods in this group furnish worthwhile amounts of protein, iron, several of the B Vitamins, and food energy.

Amounts recommended: Choose four servings or more daily. Or, if no cereals are chosen, have an extra serving of breads or baked goods, which will make at least five servings from this group daily.

Count as one serving one slice of bread, one ounce ready-to-eat cereal, ½ to ¾ cup cooked cereal, cornmeal, grits, macaroni, noodles, rice, or spaghetti.[7]

When buying the basic four—and other items—buy advertised specials first.

With *all* purchases, buy private labels (house brands) rather than national label brands. A sack full of national label brand items costs $24.58. The same items sold under house-brand labels cost $16.20.

The attached chart shows how much you save on twenty-one house-brand items.

Item	National Name Brand	Private House Brand	You Save
12 oz. can frozen orange juice	$ .67	$ .57	$ .10
1 lb. box salted crackers	.59	.49	.10
1 lb. coffee	3.26	3.09	.19
4 lb. box powdered milk	5.15	4.21	.16
1 lb. spaghetti	.48	.34	.09
30 oz. can fruit cocktail	.72	.65	.07
16 oz. can peas	.41	.34	.07
16 oz. can tomatoes	.81	.59	.22
5 lbs. flour	1.09	.89	.13
5 lbs. sugar	.99	.95	.04
3 lbs. shortening	1.95	1.79	.16
2 lb. 8 oz. jar peanut butter	2.19	1.75	.44

14 oz. bottle ketchup	.53	.45	.08
1 lb. 4 oz. loaf bread	.65	.55	.10
10 ¾ oz. can tomato soup	.22	.17	.05
½ gallon ice cream	1.59	1.19	.40
four-roll pack toilet tissue	.97	.79	.18
1 qt. jar mayonnaise	1.43	.99	.44
1 lb. 1 oz. box laundry soap	1.59	1.19	.40
box of 24 disposable diapers (over 11 lb. babies, daytime)	2.56	2.15	.41

(Same region, same time, same store chain.)

Carefully examine ads and posters screaming, "Special," "This Week Only," "Compare," and "Why Pay More?" None say the product is cheap. The slogans are like Shakespeare's "full of sound and fury, signifying nothing." Beware of other super-tricks of supermarkets.

Don't snatch end-of-aisle sales. They're *not* sales, because (1) You don't need them. Most end-of-aisle sales are pastry, cookies, and other junk foods. (2) The *same* item (under a different label) may actually cost less *even though it is not on sale.* However, you will have to hunt for those items, whereas the so-called sale items (an expensive national brand, say) are right there crowding you in the aisle.

Here is the store's strategy: 24 ozs. of Brand X beans, marked 87¢ and stacked on end-of-aisle, is tagged "Sale." Last week, you see, 24 ozs. of Brand X beans (same item, same label, same store) were 89¢. In comparison to 89¢ the 87¢ "sale" price does indeed appear to be a sale. Now, if you hunt among the shelves of beans, you'll find on the bottom shelf a 24-oz. can of beans—Brand Y beans—for 73¢. It has always been there and it has always been cheaper than Brand X. And it is still cheaper at 73¢—14¢ cheaper than the "sale" price of Brand X at 87¢.

Beware of signs like "Look, 2 for ——," or "Today Only, 3 for ——," etc. They are no guarantee of a sale. Here's why: suppose an 8½ oz. can of tomato paste (normally 24¢) is advertised as "Today's Best Buy, 3 for 89¢." That's over 29¢ per can and, clearly, *not* a sale.

Beware of the brightly packaged, eye-level items, frequently the high mark-up and unnecessary items. Low mark-up items, drably wrapped, are usually staple items which the store tucks into lower shelves. They know you'll hunt for them. They don't have to waste eye-grabbing, eye-level shelf space for items you need.

Beware of sale items sold as a "package" with nonsalable items. A genuine sale is frequently placed next to a high priced item, and a recipe, calling for both, is conveniently placed on the same rack. *The Progressive Grocer* coaches its manager-readers, for example, to place on sale cauliflower next to high-priced cheese and to stack cauliflower-cheese dish recipes between the two items. To increase pressure on the shopper, a picture of the tempting dish accompanies the recipe.

Beware of impulsiveness. Count to ten before placing in your shopping basket any questionable item. Or tell yourself you'll come back to it after you've purchased everything else. Both strategies will protect you from impulsive, wasteful purchases.

Use your prearranged floor plan. Otherwise you'll be lured to those many displays which tempt you to buy what you don't need.

Look at *all* prices on *all* sizes. Some supermarkets, aware that cautious shoppers ordinarily buy larger-sized packages (usually cheaper, ounce for ounce), use the tactic of adding *more* mark-up to the larger-sized packages. They assume the shopper will say to himself, "I'll just pick up this larger size. They are always cheaper." The shopper, therefore, doesn't compare ounce-for-ounce prices. He buys the high mark-up items, and the store gets richer. I once, for example, picked up a 2-lb. box of brown sugar priced at 49¢. I nearly bought it. To be sure, however, I compared it to a 1-lb. box. It was priced at 23¢. I bought two of the one pound.

Using your pocket calculator, or pen and pad, total as you shop. Know the exact amount before you check out. Keep an eye on the register as purchases are rung up. If the final total does not square with yours, find out why. Dishonest stores use many tricks to rip-off our money. Here's one. They place on the corner of the check-out counter some common item—a pound of coffee at $3.89, for example. They then ring up the coffee with *your* purchases—and everyone else's. The coffee is left in the corner of the check-out table after each set of purchases is rung up and bagged. Meanwhile the store (or individual clerk who may be making fast money for himself) continues to collect an extra $3.89 for each customer coming through. If a customer should notice that his bill is $3.89 too high, the clerk innocently says, "Oh, isn't that coffee yours?" For *that* customer (the alert one) the store refunds $3.89 or bags the coffee, should the customer decide to keep it. The store then simply shoves another 1-lb. can in the corner and starts the rip-off all over again.

Don't let them steal, cheat, or make errors on you. Remember, you're running a business. If your business loses money, *you* lose money. And you eat oatmeal or beans for several days until the new paycheck comes in.

Wherever possible, buy items in returnable containers. In the long run, it's not only cheaper but better for the environment.

Always return defective food, regardless of how much or how little is left. If you've eaten nearly a jar of peanut butter or drunk a gallon of milk, and you spot chips of plastic or other debris glittering in the bottom, take the whole container back. A reputable store will refund your money or give you a fresh jar. If they won't, write or call the president of the company. (Ralph Nader advises consumers to shoot complaints right to the top.)

Saving Money on Buying, Preparing the Basic Four

Breads and Cereals

Find a bakery with a day-old discount or thrift-store section. Buy twenty loaves at a time, providing your freezer has room. You save money and frequent trips to the store which saves gas money and wear and tear on the car. A 1½-lb. loaf of fresh bread runs 50¢-60¢ per loaf. The same 1½-oz. loaf, *day-old*, runs 20¢-25¢ per loaf. For the price of two loaves of fresh bread, you can buy up to five loaves of day-old. Incidentally, if you buy fresh bread, it's usually a couple of days before the whole loaf is eaten—and then it's day-old.

Beware of the temptations in the day-old store to load up on piles of day-old doughnuts, danish, cookies, and snack-cakes. You're tempted to think, "Well, I'm saving so much on day-old bread, I can afford to splurge and buy a few treats." You *can't* afford it. You're running a business. And if you're not disciplined in your spending, you'll end up buying piles of junk foods and lose any savings you gained on the day-old bread. Your business will suffer.

Eat heels of bread first, before they get too dry. Never throw away dry bread, including heels or bread crusts. Scold people who do.

Use stale bread for French toast, bread pudding, stuffings, and hard toast to break into croutons for salads and soups. Soak very stale bread in milk and feed it to pets, or take it to the zoo and feed it to the animals (many zoos will let you), or to the park and feed it to the ducks and pigeons (makes a nice walk for you and the kids too).

Cereal: "Fifty kinds of cereal stacked half-way up the wall. Who needs this jungle?!" screamed one shopper. We don't need it. But the stack grows higher and glows brighter. The cereal-sellers prey on kids, like the wicked witch preying on Snow White's gullibility.

Before you leave the house to shop, explain to your children that "we don't have enough money to buy Crunchies, Sweeties, Yummies" and other coated breakfast goo. Tell them that the money you'll save by not buying Crunchies, etc., you'll give to poor people (poorer than you). Be sure you do it, and let them see you do it.*

You may have to remind the children in the store about the need for saving money. Talking to them before you leave the house, however, gives you and them added protection from being overwhelmed by the jungle.

Some cereals are all right if you buy selectively. Prices vary

---

*Write World Vision, Box O, Pasadena, California. Ask them to send you a Love Loaf bank. Set it on your table and drop in the change you (kids too) have saved through tough spending. When it is full, send the bank back to World Vision who'll directly use it to feed the world's hungry.

enormously. A family of five eating from "variety-pack" individual cartons gets ten servings (each)—a total of fifty servings—for $9.49. The family, eating cooked cereal, gets ten servings each—a total of fifty servings—for $1.25.

Lay off sugared cereals entirely. Besides ruining teeth and putting on empty calories, it costs about 6¢ per serving. Unsweetened dry cereals cost about 3¢ per serving; cooked cereals about 1½¢ per serving.

Dairy Products

Milk: Buy powdered milk in large boxes. It will keep for a long time if container is kept closed and dry. A quart of fresh milk costs about 40¢, powdered, 20¢. If you tire of its taste, add a dab of vanilla or chocolate. If you use chocolate, don't use the expensive "Instant Chocolate Drink" mixes. Instead, mix cocoa half and half with sugar, dissolve with a touch of hot water (tap water will do) and add three, four or five tablespoons of powdered milk to make one glass (to taste).

If family members just don't like the taste of powdered milk, try this: Keep three gallon-size jars in the refrigerator. Label one "Powdered Milk" (or simply "P.M."), for cooking; the other two jars for drinking milk. Buy one gallon of whole milk, pour half into each jar and fill the remaining half with powdered milk. It tastes fine and gives you two good gallons of drinking milk for the price of one.

When you buy fresh milk, buy in returnable jugs. For an even better bargain for your milk dollar, look for milk stamped U.S. EXTRA GRADE.

Another way of saving is to find a cow. Unless you happen to live in the middle of Manhattan, choked with tenements and office buildings, you can always find someone in surrounding areas who has milk cows and will sell fresh milk directly. (Even thirty miles outside Manhattan dairy cows graze.) Frequently the owner will be glad to sell the milk (cheap) since his family can't possibly consume the eight gallons of milk given by one cow each day.

Instead of whipping cream or the various "Cold-Whip" preparations in plastic bowls and aerosol cans, use canned milk. When well-chilled, canned milk whips up thick and rich. Before whipping, put bowls and beaters in freezer for a few minutes. The colder the milk, beaters, and bowl, the faster and thicker the milk whips, Add sugar to taste as you whip.

Instead of sour cream on baked potatoes, use buttermilk. You'll find the same tart taste, with much less cost.

Don't waste money by letting milk spoil. Store milk and all dairy products (except ice cream, which is stored best at 0°-10°) at 30°-40° F. At 30°, milk will keep about twenty-four days; at 40°, about ten days. Storage time drops rapidly as storage temperature drops: at 45°, milk will keep about five days; at 50°, about two days; at 60°, about one day; at 70°, one-half day.

Eggs: Scan yellow pages and classified ads for poultry farms that sell direct. If duck eggs are cheaper than chicken eggs where you live, buy them. Usually larger than chicken eggs, they cook exactly the same as chicken eggs and taste nearly the same.

Don't wait for Easter to add food-coloring to hard boiled eggs. You won't have to harass your kids to eat their necessary quota of eggs. They'll gobble up the blue, orange, and purple "Easter eggs."

Margarine/butter: Buy in pound blocks and cut into quarters yourself. When on sale, buy several and freeze.

Meat

The best way to save money on meat is not to eat it. You'll not only save money but also your health. *Today's Health, the magazine of the American Medical Association, says:*

> The average American has been conditioned to believe that only a meat-based diet can provide the nutrition necessary for good health. Traditionally, we are a nation of carnivores, consuming some fifteen pounds of meat per person per month. (The Japanese, by contrast, eat only about a half pound, per person, per month.) Does this great U.S. "meat gorge" make nutritional sense? *Is* meat necessary to our health? [8]

Apparently, it's not; but its *protein* is. But when we consume a great amount of meat simply to get protein, we get more than we asked for:

> . . . The primary problem most American meat eaters face is not a deficiency of protein (most of us get all we need, and then some), but an excess of calories, because the meat we eat is so larded with saturated fat.

The fat not only adds to the meat for which we pay dearly but also adds unwelcome and dangerous weight to us:

> Most meat eaters . . . consistently exceed their limits in calories and, as a consequence, tend to weigh more. "Forty per cent of the fat in our diets comes from meat," says Dr. Frederick Stare, chairman of the department of nutrition at the Harvard School of Public Health. "This fat is heavily—about 40 per cent—of the saturated, cholesterol-producing variety."

There are cheaper and less fattening ways to get the protein we need. Compare the varieties in the following chart, composed by First National City Bank of New York:

WHAT PROTEIN COSTS

Here is what twenty grams of protein—or one-third the adult daily need—costs in the form of different foods.

Dried lima beans	7¢
Peanut butter	12¢
Cottage cheese	14¢
Chicken	17¢
American processed cheese	17¢
Ocean perch fillet, frozen	20¢
Milk	21¢
Eggs	22¢
Tuna fish	23¢
Hamburger	23¢
All meat frankfurters	33¢
Rib roast of beef	58¢
Sirloin steak	70¢

Overall, meat is the most expensive way to eat protein. That doesn't mean you have to vow to become a vegetarian; it means you should buy and prepare meat stingily—very stingily.

Sidney Margoulis, family-finance columnist, says:

> In food, families are most likely to overspend for meats and prepared food. Meat, of course, is important, but its flavor can be extended with other foods. It may pay you to find out how much of your food money actually goes for meat. If your total spending for meat . . . runs over 25-30 cents of your food dollar, you can consider that a warning signal.[9]

Here are a few ways to stretch your money on beef, chicken, pork, cold cuts, fish, and other meat.

Beef: You already know that the cheapest beef product is hamburger. You should also know the following:

Don't buy "hamburger-helping," "skillet-mix" dishes to go with hamburger. The ingredients in the mixes you can buy separately and fix your own hamburger dishes.

Buy hamburger marked *TVP* (textured vegetable protein). You ought to know about TVP:

> Textured vegetable proteins are manufactured from defatted soybean flour or meal by a complicated process of spinning or extrusion that gives them a fibrous texture similar to cooked meat. They come in granules, bits, dices and chunks and in beef, ham and chicken flavors or unflavored. High in protein, they have no cholesterol, and little, if any, fat.[10]

Not only does TVP add body and appearance to hamburger but it also trims hamburger's price. One supermarket describes how TVP trims hamburger's price:

> By combining one pound of 75% lean ground beef with two-thirds cup of TVP, you wind up with 23 ounces of combined mixture at a cost of 72 cents a pound verses 93 cents for ground beef alone, a saving of 22%. When ground beef sells for $1.19 a pound, the difference between beef and beef plus soy protein climbs to 29¢, for a saving of 24%.

And TVP is better for you:

> Dr. Aaron M. Altschul, professor in the School of Medicine at Georgetown University, suggests that eating high-quality soy protein foods with no cholesterol and little fat may reduce the risk of some of the diseases associated with high-cholesterol and fat consumption. And Dr. Jean Mayer, professor of nutrition at

Harvard, wrote that textured vegetable proteins, when combined with meat, fish, or poultry are nutritionally better, since proteins have a way of 'boosting' each other combined in the right way.

The *Changing Times* article suggests, "Considering their economic and health benefits, maybe you ought to begin working out some recipes that include them."

The cheapest way to prepare hamburger is in casseroles and meat loaves (recipes for both are in the recipe section). Make several casseroles and meat loaves at a time and freeze. That's cheaper *and easier* in the long run. Add nutrition, taste, and quantity to plain hamburger patties by adding ¼ cup applesauce to each pound of hamburger.

When your appetite for roast beef or steak gets overwhelming and you surrender, do *not* surrender by buying frozen beef dinners. They cost 23% more than beef dinners prepared at home. And don't satisfy your beef hunger in a restaurant. For the cost of a steak dinner or roast beef dinner in a restaurant, you can buy a stack of beef or steaks in a supermarket. (See recipe section for low cost beef dinners.)

If you're really aggressive about saving money on beef, search newspapers and scout surrounding farm areas for someone who raises beef cows. Buy a small cow or calf directly from the owner and take to the slaughter house yourself. Rent or borrow a pickup or car van. It needs to be a small cow or calf because a large cow slaughtered and dressed fills several freezers. Here's the cost savings: on say, a 400-lb. calf (about average), the calf costs about 48¢ a lb. on the hoof. It costs about another 8¢ to have it slaughtered and dressed. That's 56¢ a lb. A calf dresses down to better than one-half its "on the hoof" weight, meaning a 400-lb. calf dresses down to slightly over 200 lbs. You pay, however, for the 400 lbs. But that is still a saving. Now, 400 lbs. at 56¢ equals $224. That's $224 for over 200 lbs. of beef or about $1 a lb. That $1 a lb. includes steak, brisket, roasts, filet as well as stew meat and hamburger. Obviously, you can't get steak and roasts, etc., for anything near $1 a lb.

If you don't have $224 to spend at one time, get several families together. And check with local farmers or Better Business Bureau to find out which slaughter houses are reputable.

Obviously, you can't buy beef directly if you don't have a freezer to put it in. Check into buying one, or share one with someone else.

Poultry: Turkey, off season, is worth looking into. In addition to eating the turkey itself, try turkey salad, turkey stew, turkey chowder, and turkey croquettes. Turkey dishes help to stretch out your meat dollar. (See recipe section.)

Whole chickens are cheaper than cut-up chickens. Buy several on sale and freeze. Like cows, chickens can be bought directly from area farmers who would be delighted to show an adventurous city dweller how to kill, pluck, and dress a chicken. Buy several chickens at a time to make your trip to the country worthwhile.

Pork: If you're fortunate enough to live in an area of the country (and there are some) where wild hogs run the woods, hunt one. Check with local department of natural resources for permit information. Wild hogs plunder pastures and farms and often eat themselves into starvation; therefore, your hunting will be well justified. Some areas have open game year round, but you do need a license. After you've caught one, it'll cost about 8¢ a lb. to slaughter and dress; 8¢ a lb. for pork chops, bacon, sausage and ham isn't bad.

Buy bacon ends in bucket. Sometimes it sells three pounds for a dollar. Not only does it contain lean pieces, but its real value is in adding flavor and body to beans and stews.

Skip sausage for breakfast. It's too expensive and adds unnecessary poundage. Substitute fried bologna or frankfurters. To add protein and taste, let bologna fry till edges curl up, fill with cottage cheese (or your favorite eggs) and tip with ring of pineapple. Part frankfurters lengthwise and fill with crumbled cheese (your choice) and top with sprinkling of Parmesan cheese.

Other meats—horsemeat: One housewife fed her family on horsemeat for a year. They never suspected it. It's good and it's cheap.

Goat: Goats are still raised in many parts of the country. Buy a couple of goats direct and have them slaughtered yourself. Barbecued goat is unbeatable. Do the same with sheep (except there are more ways to fix mutton than goat).

Deer: Some states have deer herds so large they eventually eat themselves into starvation. Hunting deer *for meat* (despite sentimental scenes of Bambi) is justified; for mere sport, it's unjustified. A full-grown deer packs hundreds of pounds of meat for a hungry family. Deer chili, steaks, roasts, and hams are thick, rich and delicious. As with wild hogs, the only cost besides hunting license and a long, cold wait on a late fall morning is the cost to have it slaughtered and dressed. Or you may slaughter it yourself: tie deer in "hanged-man" position from a tree and peel the skin off from the neck down. Then carve out the large sections of meat, beginning from shoulder area. Wash meat. Gather meat ends and pieces to run through grinder for chili meat.

Pork and beef liver are especially good fried with onions or marinated in French dressing, dipped in eggs and bread and fried in deep fat.

Fish: If you live near the Atlantic or Pacific coast, go directly to the docks and buy fish as they are brought in. It is much cheaper and fresher that way. Of course, you can also get out and fish yourself. There are a lot of books and old salts who'll tell you how to do that. I can't. I'm not a fisherman.

Vegetables and Fruits (Produce)

Grow your own vegetables and fruit. If you have the patience and sweat, a vegetable garden and fruit trees will pay for themselves over and over. A 20 x 30 garden plot—not much larger than many living rooms—yields 400 lbs. of potatoes in a year. (A booklet on gardening is listed in the back.)

If you don't have a place to grow a garden, find one. Check newspapers, check surrounding rural areas until you find a place to rent, lease, buy, or borrow. Ask your city, your church, a local business or any local club to start a plot-leasing program. Or simply get a group of neighbors together. The town of Barrington, Rhode Island, for example, in possession of several acres of rich land, leased out 20 x 30 plots to town residents (and later to out-of-town residents) for $10 a year.

In New York City area residents tried farming at home. The *New York Times* said:

> Garbage-littered lots, many of them in the worst sections of New York City, will become vegetable gardens under a program to green the city by creating a thousand farms in low-income neighborhoods.
>
> Residents of these areas, mostly young people, but some of them elderly, will do the farming—and keep the food—under the guidance of experts with the Cornell University

Cooperative. The program is financed with $500,000 from the Federal Department of Agriculture.

"The whole idea," said Albert Harris, who heads the Cornell staff, "will be to let the people in the communities do the work. It will be their gardens. We will act as consultants."

The Cornell staff will supply expertise on soil and how to improve it. The program will provide tools and fertilizer, and will pay for the rental of any necessary vehicles.

In the Bedford-Stuyvesant section of Brooklyn, Joan Edwards, the executive director of the Magnolia Tree Earth Center, which has been seccessful in working the community groups in creating vegetable gardens in littered lots, was enthusiastic about the program.

"We will not only be able to have more gardens in our own area," she said; "we may be able to expand the work into other parts of Brooklyn."

In the South Bronx, Jack Flanagan, the director of operations for the Bronx Frontier Development Corporation, said 25 community groups in the area were already interested in the program.

"We will be the liaison between the communities and Cornell," he said. "We don't want to build expectations too high, but it seems an excellent idea."

Experts in nutrition are equally pleased with the program. Joan Dye Gussow, associate professor of nutrition and education, who directs a program in nutrition at Teacher's College of Columbia University, said: "I think it's a terrific idea. When you've grown a vegetable, it's hard not to eat it. I think a lot of people have stopped eating vegetables because they've forgotten what fresh vegetables taste like."

The program is scheduled to begin officially on May 8, at a large lot in Brooklyn on Baltic Street, from Fourth to Fifth Avenue, where a sort of neighborhood garbage dump is to be converted this summer into a community vegetable farm.

However, preliminary work has already begun there, with youngsters clearing the ground to get the earth ready for the seed.

In this, and all other vegetable gardens in the program, the community will get the food. Cornell will have nutrition and agricultural experts available for the community workers, who may be undecided about which crop to plant.

One reason the official opening will be in Brooklyn is that one of the main sponsors of the Congressional legislation that made this program possible was Representative Fred W. Richmond of Brooklyn, a member of the Appropriations subcommittee of the House Appropriations Committee.

Five other cities will have similar programs this summer under the legislation that will call for an expenditure of $1.5 million. The other cities are Los Angeles, Chicago, Philadelphia, Detroit and Houston.

"This is a step to improve urban blight," Representative Richmond said. "There are lots of areas that are just rubble, and nothing is being done about it. The people who work on such projects will feel a pride in their community. We are relating a Federal growing program to New York City."

The average farm in last summer's experiment by Cornell was 1,800 square feet, and the farmers included 135 adults and 283 youngsters. The successful farms, the Cornell study showed, had good yields of tomatoes, peppers, radishes, collard greens, zucchini, egg plant and an assortment of beans.

Mr. Ameroso, who was in charge of last year's pilot project, said most soil in city lots was "pretty acid." He said it was worse where the lots had been covered by brick buildings than where they once supported wooden houses.

Last summer's experience showed that urban farmers tend to be stingy with water. They see the ground is wet and assume that is enough.

"We will be holding classes with them in the fields or at community centers," Mr. Ameroso said. "They will learn how to poke their hands or a stick into the earth to see that the water has gone 12 inches or so."

Mr. Harris said some community groups were planning to plant a single crop because it would be easier to share among the farmers—or to sell and share the proceeds.

"We hope, no matter what they plant," he said, "that they will realize what farmers have to do to grow a crop."

Changing Times tells the story of what one church did:

In 1972 the Rev. Wilbert Staudenmaier, pastor and once a farmer, suggested to his parishioners and their friends the idea of a big family garden. He found some land and arranged to have it cultivated and planted by the owner, ready for nature and some willing hands to do the rest of the job. That year 259 families paid $5 apiece for the use of 1,000 square foot plots. Each family was responsible for weeding that could not be done by machinery and for harvesting their crops. Large families saved over $1 a day on their yearly food bills. In 1973, more than 1,500 families signed up, and the rental fee was raised to $10 so that the project could also make a profit for the church.[12]

Here is what one business did, with enthusiastic response and abundant results:

Hal Booth, president of First National Bank, read about Father Staudenmaier's project and liked the idea. Last spring the bank announced that it would sponsor a rent-a-garden project with plots of 1,000 square feet leasing for $10 each. The bank would plant, water when necessary, machine weed and provide hail insurance. Gardeners would be responsible for close weeding and harvesting. Booth thought that about 1,500 people would sign up, but over 2,263 individuals and families joined the plan and gardened over 100 acres. Only 13 lot renters failed to tend their plots. Each garden yielded about $300 worth of vegetables. The Winger family were among the Iowa gardeners, and in addition to the abundant crop of fresh produce they ate, Mrs. Jenny Winger canned 240 jars of vegetables.

If you can't grow your own, pick your own. Watch the newspapers and drive to adjacent rural areas asking local farmers where you can pick fruits and vegetables directly. It saves farmers the work and expense of picking, cleaning, hauling and selling. They'll probably charge a low fee. Strawberry farmers, for example, may charge 25¢ a basket if you come and pick your own. A similar basket in the supermarket costs three times as much.

Wholesale your own: If you can't grow or pick your own, buy your own direct from wholesalers. "But they won't sell to me!" That's right—if there's just one of you.

In Washington, D.C. (and other areas), a dozen families formed a neighborhood produce co-op. They contributed $10 a week. Each week a different family went to the wholesalers and bought approximately $120 worth of fruit and vegetables in the required large crates and cartons. Upon returning home, the shopper-family for that week divided up the produce in individual bags and boxes for each family. A lot of work? Yes. But each family was required to do the shopping and bagging only once every twelve weeks. The freshness, abundance, and cheapness of the fresh produce kept co-op families enthusiastic about the project. Rarely could they afford grapes, cherries, peaches, sweet corn, but with co-op prices, they did. For $10 each in the co-op, they got $20 worth of fresh produce.*

---

*If you want to go into wholesale food buying in a big way, see *How to Start Your Own Food Co-op: A Guide to Wholesale Buying* by Gloria Stern, Walker and Company, 1975.

Whether you grow, pick, or wholesale your own, you'll need to learn how to properly can and freeze produce (and all food). The United States Department of Agriculture puts out the following helpful books: *Home Canning of Fruits and Vegetables; Home Canning of Meat and Poultry; Home Freezing of Fruits and Vegetables; How to Make Jellies, Jams and Preserves at Home; Home Freezing of Poultry; Freezing Meat and Fish in the Home; Making Pickles and Relishes at Home; Freezing Combination Main Dishes.* Write: Office of Communications, U.S.D.A., Washington, D.C. 20250.

Produce in the supermarket: Buy institution-sized cans of fruits and vegetables. Generally the larger the can, the less the per-unit price. This is generally true, but not always; therefore, check the ounces and price on every purchase. For example, a 30-oz. can of tomato sauce at 35¢ is obviously *not* cheaper than two 16-oz. cans at 17¢ each. Check ounces and prices on every purchase. Don't buy canned fruits or vegetables simply because they are on sale. Three cans of pickled cauliflower for 89¢ is no sale if no one in the house eats it.

Buy lower grade canned goods. Grade A is fancy, B is choice, C is standard. Buy grade C. Grades are based on color, texture, flavor, shape, uniformity, and freedom from defects—not on nutritional content.

Don't buy packets of instant vegetables. The more preparation required to put a product on a shelf the more expensive it is.

And don't buy canned or packaged if the fresh is available. Compare the per serving costs of potatoes:

Fresh potatoes . . . . $.02 per serving
Instant potatoes . . . . .03 -.04 per serving
Frozen potatoes . . . . .05 per serving
Canned potatoes . . . . .06 per serving
Frozen french fries . . . . .10 per serving
Frozen stuffed . . . . .11 per serving

Before shopping for fresh produce, call the local Home Extension Service, State Department of Agriculture, or similar office to ask what fruits and vegetables are in season. In-season fruits and vegetables are cheaper.

Keep fresh fruit and vegetables in produce bin of refrigerator to protect taste and texture.

The cheapest canned vegetables usually are beans, butter beans, spinach (rich in Vitamins A and C, too), tomatoes, and sometimes waxed beans. But buy in institution-sized cans and divide contents into freezer bags. (See section on freezing.)

Preparing fruits and vegetables cheaply: Mix lentils with other foods. They are cheap, protein rich and can be grown in your own house. Mix soybeans with other foods—another cheap, nutritional supplement. Eat parsley and don't use it merely for decoration. Buy carrots fresh; then cook and freeze.

Prepare vegetable dishes with grits. They are cheap, flexible, and filling. Or prepare baked grits. (See recipes.) It makes a delicious dish. Use tops of green onions in salads or soups. Cook beet and radish tops with other greens. Beet tops, by themselves, may be cooked like spinach. With a touch of sour cream (or whipped buttermilk) and a dash of horseradish, they're delicious.

Make patties of left-over mashed potatoes and fry for breakfast. Add a pat of jelly.

Use left-over rice, noodles, and boiled potatoes for soups and stews. Put tarnished (not spoiled) celery leaves, lettuce leaves and carrot tops in soups and stews. Use water from vegetable cans in soups, stews and gravies. It's a vitamin-laden liquid. Use the water in which beans have been soaked as a base for soups and stews. If vegetables become so bad that they are inedible even in stews, use for garden compost.

The cheapest canned fruits, usually, are applesauce, fruit cocktail, peaches and plums.

Thin and warm up juice from canned fruits and use for pancake syrup and/or pudding topping. Also mix half and half with mayonnaise for a delicious dressing on fruit salads. Or you may thicken with cornstarch for a cake sauce. Combine with brown sugar and thicken with cornstarch as a sauce for ham. Use fruit syrup instead of water when you make jello desserts. Or combine fruit syrup with a dab of margarine and ¼ cup brown sugar as a tasty glaze on cooked whole carrots.

A Word on Desserts

Gelatin dishes, "Jello" dishes and puddings are cheap and often nutritious desserts. Coffee jello, made from left-over coffee, and bread pudding and rice pudding, made from left-over bread and rice, are especially cheap.

Cakes and cookies that you make yourself are, generally, the cheapest kinds. Make large sheet cakes. Occasionally, you'll find cake mixes cheaper than homemade. Buy several boxes and save them for those special occasions when you want cake for dessert. If cookies (or crackers) wilt, losing their "snap," put on large cookie sheet and place in oven for a few minutes. Heat will restore their crispness.

Carbonated sodas drill your teeth, fatten your belly, and drain your wallet. For the price of a dozen cans of soda, you can buy a sturdy ice jug, with spigot, which you can fill and refill ad infinitum with cheap kool-aid or cheaper ice water. (Whatever happened to water, just plain water, as America's favorite drink?)

Overall, the best thing to do about desserts and sweets is skip them. You'll save not only your money but also your body from superfluous intake of sugar. Or, if that seems too brutal, cut desserts to once or twice a week. (Makes them more special that way.) Try getting into the habit of providing (in-season) fresh fruit at the end of meals, instead of sweets, for dessert.

For that rare and special occasion, when you want a special dessert, check the dessert section for inexpensive, good desserts.

Saving Money on Staples

Buy sugar in a 25-lb. sack. If your local supermarket does not carry it, find a refinery nearby.

Buy flour in 25-lb. sacks or 50-lb. sacks (especially important since price of flour has just gone up 1.6¢ again following the Russian wheat deal). To insure that stored flour does not get infested with weevils, put flour in smaller plastic bags or well-sealed paper bags and store in the freezer.

Buy pasta (spaghetti, macaroni, etc.) products in larger-sized packages. *Don't* wash pasta before cooking else you lose nutritional content.

Use lard, with a dash of salt, instead of shortening (makes delicious pie crust, among other things).

Don't buy instant rice and instant potato products.

Saving Money on Paper Goods and Toiletries

Generally, you should buy paper goods and toiletries in a mammoth discount store, rather than a supermarket.

But don't buy "wax paper," "plastic wrap," and "aluminum foil" products. Save the inside wrappings of cereal, cookie and cracker, etc. boxes instead. (Frequently, the wrapping is heavy-duty waxed paper or foil; better than the rolls of waxed paper you would ordinarily buy.) Save bread wrappers to use for wrapping sandwiches, lunch sacks, and freezer bags.

Don't buy paper towels. Almost anything you can do with a paper towel, you can do with an old rag, at much less expense.

If paper boy delivers your paper wrapped in string or rubber bands, you are in luck. Save rubber bands and string; it'll considerably reduce your need to buy them.

Save cotton from medicine bottles. Women will find it useful for cosmetic purposes.

Be very conservative about any toiletries bought in an aerosol can. Frequently, the cost of the *can* exceeds the cost of the contents.

Don't buy shaving cream. Ordinary hand soap lathers well enough to give a good shave.

Saving Money Here 'n There

Cook less food, serve less food—make them ask for more. That's cheaper than piling a mountain of food on the table, enticing everyone to eat more than he really needs. If you do cook too much, serve the leftovers at the next meal, or freeze. (See *Freezing* section.) Never, never, never throw food away.

Date foods you put into the freezer.

Forget big lunches. Many of us don't need them, and they add weight, money, and sluggishness to our days. There is no way you can eat a fat lunch, return to a sitting job, and remain alert and awake. A piece of fruit, a few peanuts, a salad, a cup of yogurt will do many people very nicely.

If you spend above your food budget, eat oatmeal until you get paid again. That will teach you to do better next time.

The cost of eating out (even at "burger factories") is much higher than you can eat at home. Run *away* from restaurants and chicken/burger/taco places. Should an emergency require you to eat out, you can save money simply by drinking water at the burger factory instead of soda or shakes and by avoiding dessert. Split hamburgers between kids. For example, a family of four at a burger factory ordering four hamburgers, four french fries, four desserts, and four Cokes or shakes spends about $8.50.

Instead, try this next time. Take one hamburger and split it between the kids (or between two overweight parents). Do the same with french fries. Drink water and skip the dessert. You'll get away with the meal for around $2.50.

Give money and food away to those who need it more than you. That's right. Part of the frustration and humiliation of living on tight wages is the lack of power and joy involved in helping others. Joy is always in giving, not in getting. Poor families, unfortunately, usually are robbed of that joy. They don't have to be.

Sounds impractical, doesn't it? But it works because God put this law in our universe: whatever *you* need, give it away.

Depressed and in need of encouragement? Give encouragement to someone else; *your* depression will vanish. Lonely and alone? Be a friend to another who is lonely; your loneliness will melt. Poor and worried? Give money to one poorer than yourself; your worry—and poverty—will fade. It's a joy and power not understood until tried.

The Psalmist said: "I have been young, and now am old; yet have I not seen the righteous forsaken, nor his seed [children] begging bread" (Ps 37:25). He was right.

Foreword to Recipes

In the beginning of her celebrated book, *Good Cheap Food*, Miriam Ungerer says:

> To the frequently asked question: "Did you make up all these recipes yourself?" the answer is "No." And neither does any other cookbook writer. Cooking is an evolutionary art proceeding simultaneously in many kitchens, and even when you do hit on something you think is original, chances are you'll find something very like it in the *Larousse Gastronomique.* I've invented some of the things in this book; others are my interpretation of classic dishes. In some instances I have adapted recipes for thrift, but never so much so that the character of the dish is ruined. (*Good Cheap Food,* Viking Press, New York, 1973, p. 6.)

I agree.

However, I adapted *no* recipes from *Good Cheap Food.* There is a reason for that.

Some cookbooks (and *Good Cheap Food* is probably less guilty than others) project pretty weird ideas about "cheap" food. For them a "cheap" recipe is one using domestic sherry instead of imported sherry, sirloin cuts instead of filet, and fresh avocadoes instead of frozen. Those *are* cheap recipes if you live in the $25,000-$50,000+ category.

The recipes in this book arose from living in the $5,000—$15,000 category. They are for Joe Lunchpail and JoAnn Budget. They're meant to keep you alive and comfortably ahead of bill collectors.

Chapter 4

Eating for Survival: 100 Recipes

One-Dish Wonders*

Casseroles with Hamburger

GROUND BEEF CASSEROLE

1   pound ground beef
1   medium onion chopped
Salt and pepper to taste
½ tsp. garlic powder
1   tsp. Worcestershire sauce
½ tsp. oregano
1   can stewed tomatoes
Grated cheese
1   small package large shell macaroni

Brown meat with onion until done, but not hard. Add all your seasonings and tomatoes. Simmer about 10 minutes. At the time you add your tomatoes and seasonings start your boiling water for the macaroni and cook as is directed on package. Drain macaroni and add to meat mixture. Pour complete mixture into casserole and sprinkle grated cheese on top. Bake at 350 degrees for about 30 minutes or until cheese is well melted. Serve with salad and garlic bread for a complete meal.

POTATO-CHIP CASSEROLE

Fry one pound hamburger with one onion, stack in layers with potato chips (2 layers of each). Pour one can hot mushroom soup over mixture. Add grated cheese. Bake in hot oven until cheese melts (400 degrees).

---

*To save money and time, prepare several one-dish meals at the same time, freeze, and keep until ready to use.

HAMBURGER PIE

1 onion (finely chopped)
1 pound hamburger
1 can green beans
1 egg
1 can tomato soup
Salt and pepper to taste
6 or 7 cooked potatoes

Brown onion in small amount of shortening, add ground beef and cook slowly until done, then add drained green beans, tomato soup; let simmer about 10 minutes. Cream potatoes, add raw egg to potatoes and beat thoroughly. Put meat mixture in a casserole, top with cream potatoes, put in oven at 375 degrees till brown.

BEEF 'N BISCUIT PIE

1 pound hamburger
½ cup chopped onion
1 (8-oz.) can tomato sauce
1 tsp. salt
1 tsp. chili powder
2 cups biscuit mix
⅔ cup milk
¼ cup vegetable oil

Brown hamburger in skillet. Add onion; cook until tender; drain fat. Add sauce, salt, chili powder; heat. Combine biscuit mix, milk, oil. Knead on floured board. Pat half the dough in 9-inch pie pan. Pour in hot filling.

Pat out remaining dough and place over filling. Crimp edge; slit top. Bake at 425 degrees for 20-25 minutes. 4-6 servings.

Meat Loaf

STUFFED MEAT LOAF

1 pound hamburger
½ cup chopped green pepper
½ cup chopped onion
1 tsp. salt
1 T. Worchestershire sauce
1 cup white bread broken into small pieces
½ cup milk
2 eggs

¼ cup fat
2 cups wholewheat bread crumbs
½ cup chopped celery
¼ tsp. black pepper
¾ cup meat stock
Nuts (optional)

Combine hamburger, green pepper, onion, salt, Worcestershire sauce, white bread, milk and one egg. Mix. Place half of mixture in bottom of greased loaf pan. Combine remaining ingredients and spread on top of meat mixture. Arrange remaining meat mixture on top of stuffing. Bake at 350 degrees 1½ hours.

Skillet/Pan Dinners

BUDGET DINNER IN A SKILLET

Brown 1 pound ground beef with 3 stalks celery, cut in diagonal slices, and 1 medium onion, cut in fairly coarse chunks. Add 2 cups left-over boiled potatoes, cut in bite-size pieces, and ½ cup left-over whole-kernel corn. Blend all with a thin white sauce and season with salt, pepper, and a whiff of marjoram. Simmer slowly 10 to 15 minutes. Since this is colorless, serve with Harvard beets and gelatin vegetable salad, milk and white cake with peach topping.

HAMBURGER STROGANOFF

1   can mushroom soup
1   pound hamburger
½   cup sliced onion
2   T. butter or margarine
½   cup sour cream
⅓   cup water

In skillet, brown meat, cook onion in butter until tender. Add remaining ingredients. Cover; simmer 45 minutes or until tender. Stir occasionally. Serve over hot cooked noodles. Serves 4.

BEEF-POTATO BOATS

All-in-one meat and potato meal. Easy! Bake 4 medium size potatoes. Meanwhile, lightly brown 1 pound hamburger and ½ cup chopped celery and 1 small onion in skillet. Drain fat. Add 1 tsp. salt, ¼ tsp. nutmeg, 1 (8-oz.) can tomato sauce with onions. Cut potatoes in half lengthwise; scoop out and reserve shells. Mash potatoes, combine with meat mixture. Fill shells; place in baking pan. Sprinkle 1 cup shredded cheddar cheese on top. Bake 15 minutes at 400 degrees. Makes 4 servings.

ONE-SKILLET CORNED BEEF DINNER

2   T. butter or margarine
6   small boiled potatoes
⅛   tsp. salt
⅛   tsp. pepper
1   (12-oz.) can corned beef, cut into 4 slices
1   (16-oz.) can sauerkraut, drained
2   cups boiled carrot slices
2   tsp. prepared horseradish
2   tsp. prepared mustard

Melt butter in a 10-inch skillet over moderately low heat (about 225 degrees). Add potatoes, sprinkle with salt and pepper and turn up heat to moderately high (about 300 degrees); cook potatoes 5 to 7 minutes, turning frequently, until outsides are crisp and lightly browned. Push potatoes to one side of skillet. Add corned beef to skillet and cook until brown and crisp on both sides. Remove skillet from heat and add sauerkraut; keep separate and do not mix them with the potatoes or corned beef. Nestle the carrots in the sauerkraut. Reduce heat to moderate (about 250 degrees); cover skillet and cook 10 minutes until sauerkraut and carrots are warmed through. Meanwhile, stir horseradish and mustard separately. Serve from skillet or transfer to a heated serving dish. Serve sauce separately. Makes 4 servings.

HAM-TURKEY PIE

4   T. butter or margarine
5   T. all-purpose flour
¼   tsp. pepper
2   cups chicken broth
1   cup diced cooked ham
1   cup diced cooked turkey
½   cup sliced mushrooms
¼   cup chopped green onion
3   T. snipped parsley
1   recipe for rice shell

In saucepan, melt butter or margarine; blend in flour and pepper. Add chicken broth all at once. Cook over medium heat, stirring constantly, till mixture thickens and bubbles. Add ham, turkey, mushrooms, onion, and parsley; mix thoroughly. Pour into prepared rich shell. Bake in 350-degree oven for 40 minutes. Let stand 5 to 8 minutes. Makes 6 servings.

To make rice shell: Combine 2½ cups cooked long-grain rice, 2 beaten eggs, 4 T. melted butter, and ⅛ tsp. pepper; mix thoroughly. Press firmly into an ungreased 9-inch pie plate.

One-Dish Pork Wonder

CHEAP HAM CASSEROLE

Preheat oven to 400 degrees.
½ cup cooking oil
½ cup very small onions; saute.
1 small can mushrooms—lower heat to simmer.
¼ cup flour (pre-sifted)
Brown flour with 1½ cups milk, stirring. Add 1 can cream of celery soup, lower heat.
Add 1 cup sharp cheese, stir until melted; simmer.
Dash black pepper
3 cups cooked cubed ham
Turn off heat. Pour into large baking dish.

Topping: Mix 1½ cups dry biscuit mix with ½ cup grated cheese. Add ⅔ cup milk until ingredients are moistened. Add 2 T. finely minced onion. Dabble on top of casserole.

CHICKEN CASSEROLE
Water
3-pound chicken
1 T. salt
8 ozs. shell macaroni
½ cup shortening
½ cup chopped onion
3 T. flour
2 tsp. salt
¼ tsp. pepper
½ tsp. basil leaves
½ tsp. oregano leaves
3 cups milk
1 package (10-oz.) frozen green peas, thawed
½ cup soft bread crumbs
4 ozs. American cheese, diced

Bring 3 quarts water to a boil in large saucepan; add chicken and cook until tender. Remove chicken and reserve broth.* Remove chicken from bones and cut into bite-sized pieces. Add 1 T. salt and enough water to reserved broth to make 3 quarts liquid; bring to boil. Gradually add macaroni so that liquid continues to boil. Cook uncovered, stirring occasionally, until tender. Drain* in colander.

Meanwhile, in large skillet heat shortening; add onion and saute until lightly browned. Add flour and remaining seasonings. Gradually add milk and stir over medium heat until sauce boils 2 minutes. Add peas and heat. Combine macaroni, chicken and sauce in 2½-quart casserole. Sprinkle with crumbs and dot with cheese. Bake in 350 degree oven for 30 minutes. Makes 6-8 servings, about 35¢ per serving.

*Save broth used for cooking macaroni and use for soup or sauces, if desired.

SPAGHETTI AND CHICKEN SKILLET

8   oz. spaghetti
½   cup butter or margarine
1   broiler-fryer, 2½ pounds, cut in serving pieces
½   cup boiling water
1   (10½-oz.) can condensed cream of chicken soup
1   (1-lb.) can small whole carrots, drained
1   medium green pepper, cut into rings
½   cup sliced stuffed olives

Cook spaghetti according to directions. Drain. Heat butter in skillet.
Add chicken and cook until browned on all sides. Remove chicken.
Drain off drippings, reserving 2 T. Add ½ cup boiling water and reserved drippings to skillet. Heat to boiling, stirring occasionally. Add
soup and stir until blended. Add spaghetti and chicken with remaining
ingredients and heat to serving temperature over low heat, stirring occasionally. Serves 4 to 6; 61¢ a serving.

CHICKEN LOAF

4   cups diced chicken (or more)
2   cups fresh breadcrumbs
1   cup cooked rice
1½ tsp. salt
3   cups milk or chicken broth (or half and half)
1   cup chopped pimento
4   eggs, well beaten

Mix all the ingredients together, adding eggs last. Pour into a greased 6-
cup baking pan or ring mold. Bake at 325 degrees for 1 hour. Serve with
mushroom sauce.

Mushroom Sauce:
¼   cup butter   1   tsp. paprika
¼   cup flour   ½   tsp. chopped parsley
1   pint chicken broth   ½   tsp. lemon juice
¼   cup cream   Salt to taste
1   (6-oz.) can sliced mushrooms

Melt the butter in saucepan. Add flour and mix well, and then add the
chicken broth. Cook, stirring constantly until thick and smooth. Add
cream, mushrooms, paprika, parsley, lemon juice, and salt. Mix and let
stand over hot water until ready to serve over chicken.

One-Dish Fish

TUNA DINNER-CAKES
1 ½ cups sifted all-purpose flour
½ tsp. salt
½ cup shortening
½ cup shredded sharp cheddar cheese
4 T. water
¼ cup shortening
¼ cup chopped onion
¼ cup thinly sliced celery
¼ cup flour
1 ¾ cups flour
2 cans (6 ½ - or 7-oz. each) tuna, drained
1 tsp. salt
Dash pepper

Combine 1 ½ cups flour and ½ tsp. salt in bowl. Cut in ½ cup shortening and cheese until uniform but coarse. Sprinkle with water, toss with fork and press into a ball. On lightly floured surface, roll out pastry about ⅛-inch thick. Cut out twelve pastry circles, 3 inches in diameter. Place on ungreased baking sheet in 425-degree oven about 15 minutes or until lightly browned.

Meanwhile, melt ¼ cup shortening in medium saucepan. Stir in onion and celery. Cook until almost tender. Stir in ¼ cup flour. Gradually add milk; cook and stir over medium heat until sauce boils 2 minutes. Stir in tuna, 1 tsp. salt and the pepper. Heat thoroughly. Using 2 pastry rounds for each serving, layer with spoonsfull of tuna mixture. Makes 6 servings, about 25¢/serving.

TUNA TETRIZONI
4 ozs. cooked spaghetti
2 cans of tuna fish
½ cup green peppers
¼ cup pimentos
1 small onion, chopped fine
½ cup water
1 can mushroom soup
1 ¾ cup sharp cheddar cheese (reserve ½ for topping)

Cook spaghetti in boiling water with salt, drain; add tuna, pimentos, pepper, onions, water, mushroom soup and cheese. Put in baking dish (greased) and bake 45 minutes at 350 degrees. The last 5 minutes sprinkle remainder of cheese over the top and put back into oven to melt.

CRUNCHY SALMON LOAF*

1 ½ cups medium white sauce
3 egg yolks, well beaten
1 (1-lb.) can salmon, drained and flaked
2 T. finely chopped onion
1 tsp. paprika
1 (3-oz.) can chow mein noodles
½ cup almonds (optional)
3 egg whites, stiffly beaten
1 ½ cups medium white sauce
Sliced hard-cooked eggs
Parsley

Combine 1 ½ cups medium white sauce and egg yolks in a large mixing bowl. Add salmon, onion, paprika, noodles, and almonds; mix well. Fold in stiffly beaten egg whites. Spoon into a greased 9 x 5 x 3-inch loaf-pan. Bake at 375 degrees for 40 to 45 minutes.

Unmold loaf on serving platter. Pour 1 ½ cups medium white sauce over loaf and garnish with sliced hard-cooked eggs and parsley. Makes 6 to 8 servings.

Rice (with Something Else) Dishes

BROCCOLI AND RICE

Saute in 1 or 2 T. margarine:
½ cup chopped onion
½ cup chopped celery
Cook 1 cup rice in salted water.
Cook 1 package chopped broccoli in salted water. Drain.
Mix rice, broccoli with:
1 can cream of chicken soup
1 can cream of mushroom soup
1 jar Cheese Whiz (small size)

Put in casserole, sprinkle with paprika. Bake at 350 degrees for 10 minutes or until bubbly.

---

*On Salmon recipes, use "Chinook" Salmon (about 1.59 lb.). Fancy red salmon costs double.

CHICKEN AND RICE

1 ½ cups uncooked rice (25 min. cooking rice)
1 or 2 raw chickens, cut up
1 stick melted butter
1 package dry onion soup
3 cups water
Salt and pepper

Place uncooked rice in bottom of large pyrex dish. Arrange chicken on top of rice. Salt and pepper chicken. Pour melted butter over chicken and sprinkle onion soup over it. Add water. Cover. Cook in 350-degree oven for 2 hours.

CHEESE AND RICE CASSEROLE

3 cups cooked regular rice
2 cups shredded cheddar cheese
2 T. finely chopped green pepper
2 eggs, beaten
1 ¼ cups milk
1 tsp. salt
Dash of cayenne pepper
½ cup buttered breadcrumbs

Alternate layers of rice, cheese, and green pepper in a greased 1 ½-quart casserole dish.

Combine eggs, milk, salt, and cayenne; pour over casserole. Sprinkle breadcrumbs over top. Bake at 350 degrees about 45 minutes or until set. Makes 6 servings.

Spaghetti Dishes

CHICKEN SPAGHETTI

1 medium chicken
1 box (16-oz.) spaghetti
1 can mushrooms or cream of mushroom soup
1 can (6-oz.) tomato paste
1 cup celery, chopped fine
1 or 2 cloves of garlic
1 green pepper, chopped
1 medium onion, chopped fine
2 T. Worcestershire sauce
2 tsp. salt
¼ tsp. black pepper

Brown chicken well on all sides. Remove to deep kettle covered with just enough boiling water to cover chicken. Add salt and pepper. Simmer, covered, 1 to 1 ¼ hours or until tender. Remove meat from broth and slice. Cook spaghetti until tender in chicken broth. Make a sauce by browning onions and garlic in 2 T. of chicken fat or butter. Add green pepper, celery, tomato paste, mushrooms. Stir 5 to 10 minutes; add Worcestershire sauce. Line pan with spaghetti, then layer of chicken, then sauce. Repeat, placing white slices of chicken on top. Sprinkle with shredded cheese, cover and cook slowly for 2 hours longer until all flavors are blended, between 200 and 300 degrees. Shred more cheese to sprinkle on top when served.

HURRY-SPAGHETTI SUPPER
Keep this recipe handy. It's a good one.

1 pound ground beef	1 tsp. salt
1 onion, chopped	1 tsp. sugar
1 minced clove garlic	½ tsp. oregano
2 (6-oz.) cans tomato paste	½ tsp. basil
3 cups water	¼ tsp. pepper

Lightly brown beef, onion and garlic; drain fat. Stir in remaining ingredients. Simmer, uncovered, one hour. Serve over hot spaghetti. Makes 4 servings.

Macaroni and Noodle Dishes

MACARONI CHICKEN SALAD
1 T. salt
3 quarts boiling water
2 cups elbow macaroni (8 ozs.)
2 cups diced cooked chicken
1 cup diced celery
2 sweet gherkins, chopped
2 T. chopped onion
1 canned pimento, chopped
⅓ cup mayonnaise
Juice of 1 medium lemon
⅛ tsp. dry mustard
Dash Tabasco sauce
1 medium tomato, cut in 8 wedges

Add 1 T. salt to rapidly boiling water. Gradually add macaroni so that water continues to boil. Cook uncovered, stirring occasionally, until tender. Drain in colander. Rinse with cold water; drain again.

Combine and toss macaroni, chicken, celery, gherkins, onion, pimento, mayonnaise, lemon juice, and seasonings. Chill. Garnish with tomato wedges.

Meat Dishes

Chicken and Turkey

CHICKEN CONTINENTAL
3-4 pound chicken pieces (thighs, legs, breasts)
⅓ cup seasoned flour
¼ cup butter
1 can cream of chicken soup
2½ T. grated onion
1 tsp. salt
1 T. chopped parsley
⅛ tsp. thyme
½ tsp. celery flakes
1⅓ cup water
1⅓ cup minute rice
½ tsp. paprika

Roll chicken in flour, saute in butter until golden brown. Mix soup, onion, seasonings in sauce pan. Gradually stir in water and bring to boil stirring constantly. Pour rice into shallow 2-quart casserole. Stir in all but ⅓ soup mixture. Top with chicken and pour on remaining soup mixture. Cover. Rice isn't boiled first so gathers up the flavors. Bake 1 hour at 375 degrees. Sprinkle with paprika.

CREAMED CHICKEN AND PEAS (6 servings)
3 T. margarine
2 T. green pepper, chopped
5 T. flour
1 chicken bouillon cube
1¼ cups water
1¼ cup reconstituted instant nonfat milk
3 cups diced cooked chicken
1 cup cooked frozen peas
1 tsp. salt
½ tsp. mace

Melt margarine in a 2-quart saucepan. Add green pepper and cook until tender. Blend in the flour. Add bouillon cube, water and milk. Cook to a smooth mixture stirring constantly. Mix in chicken, peas, salt, and mace. Heat mixture thoroughly. Approximate cost per serving 57 cents.

FOIL-BAKED CHICKEN

(With this always-perfect chicken barbecue you'll have no grill or broiler pan to clean.)

½ cup water
⅓ cup catsup
⅓ cup vinegar
¼ cup brown sugar
4   T. butter or margarine, melted
2   T. Worcestershire sauce
2   T. lemon juice
2   tsp. salt
2   tsp. paprika
2   tsp. chili powder
2   tsp. dry mustard
2   broiler-fryers, 2½ to 3 pounds each, cut up

In bowl, blend together all ingredients except chicken. Dip chicken pieces in sauce. Divide chicken in 4 to 6 serving-size portions, placing each serving on separate piece of heavy foil. Pour about 1 T. sauce over each portion of chicken; seal foil securely. Bake in 400-degree oven for 45 minutes. Open foil packets; brush with remaining sauce. Bake 15 minutes. Makes 4 to 6 servings.

PEPPERED CHICKEN

2   whole chicken breasts
3   small green peppers
1   pound small onions, peeled
1   can (10¾ oz.) condensed chicken broth, undiluted
½   cup water
2   T. cornstarch
1   tsp. salt
6   T. pure vegetable oil
1   clove of garlic, crushed
½   pound spaghetti, cooked and deep-fried* or 3 cans (3 ozs. each) chow mein noodles

Rinse chicken; skin and bone. Cut chicken into 1-inch chunks. Cut peppers in half; remove seeds and membranes; cut into strips. Cut onions into narrow wedges. Combine chicken broth, water, cornstarch and salt in small bowl. Heat 2 T. oil in kettle or Dutch oven over high heat. Add peppers, onions and garlic. Cook 2 minutes, stirring quickly and constantly with slotted spoon. Remove vegetables to bowl. Heat 2 more T. oil in pan. Add half the chicken. Cook 5 minutes or until lightly browned, stirring occasionally. Remove to bowl. Brown other half of chicken in remaining oil. Return chicken and vegetables to pan. Stir cornstarch mixture; add to chicken. Bring to boiling, stirring constantly. Spoon over fried spaghetti or canned noodles on platter. Makes 6 servings.

Turkey

Turkey Basics

Choosing and cooking turkey can be baffling. To simplify both jobs, check these pointers before turkey time.

Types: There are several kinds of birds to buy. Dressed, ready-to-cook, quick frozen turkeys are the most plentiful and come packed in airtight plastic bags.

Some people prefer fresh-chilled turkeys which have never been frozen but are somewhat more expensive.

---

*To deep-fry cooked spaghetti, toss cooked spaghetti with a T. oil to keep the strands separated. Pour enough fat or pure vegetable oil in kettle to make ⅓ full. Heat to 370 degrees. Lower small amount of spaghetti into oil. Fry until crisp, turning once. Remove. Drain on paper towels. Repeat until all spaghetti is fried.

You may choose a self-basting turkey. These birds have had fat injected beneath the skin in the breast and leg areas.

Turkey hindquarters include the leg, thigh, part of the back, piece of wing, and some giblets. They are great for small families who like dark meat.

Turkey roll roasts with both light and dark meat are also available. They range in size from two to six pounds and can be purchased plain or with gravy.

Servings: The number of servings per bird depends somewhat upon the size of appetites in your family. A homemaker can plan a pound per person when selecting a whole turkey or five ounces per serving for a boneless turkey roll. This gives everyone a generous serving plus some leftovers.

Preparation: Thaw turkey in the original moisture-proof wrapping in the refrigerator. Or, you can thaw by placing the wrapped bird in a pan of cool water; change water often. (Warm or hot water will raise the temperature of the outside of the bird too quickly.)

Ready-to-Cook Weight	Approximate Time in Refrigerator	Approximate Time in Water Bath
3 to 8 pounds	1 to 2 days	3 to 5 hours
8 to 12 pounds	1 to 2 days	5 to 7 hours
12 to 20 pounds	2 to 3 days	7 to 9 hours

After thawing, free legs and tail from tucked position. Remove bird from bag. Remove neck and giblets. Refrigerate within 24 hours after thawing.

Turkey Roasting Chart

325-degree oven

Purchased ready-to-cook weight	Guide to total roasting time*
6 to 8 pounds	3 ½ to 4 hours
8 to 12 pounds	4 to 4 ½ hours

*If turkey is unstuffed, less roasting time may be required.

12 to 16 pounds	4½ to 5½ hours
16 to 20 pounds	5½ to 6½ hours
20 to 24 pounds	6½ to 7½ hours

To Roast Whole Turkey

Preheat oven to 325 degrees. First, rinse thawed bird; pat dry. Stuff wishbone cavity; skewer neck skin to back. Tuck wing tips behind shoulder joints. Rub salt in body cavity; lightly fill with stuffing. Push drumsticks under band of skin at tail (or tie to tail). Brush bird with melted cooking fat. Insert meat thermometer in center of inside thigh muscle, making sure bulb does not touch bone. Place turkey, breast side up, on rack in a shallow roasting pan. Cover with a loose "cap" of foil. Avoid having foil touch top or sides of the turkey.

When turkey is two-thirds done, according to chart, cut band of skin or cord at tail so heat can reach inside of thighs. Continue cooking till meat thermometer registers 185 degrees. The thickest part of drumstick should feel very soft when pressed between fingers protected with paper toweling; the turkey's drumstick should move up and down and twist easily in socket.

To Roast in Covered Pan

Preheat oven to 350 degrees. Prepare bird as above and insert meat thermometer. Place turkey, breast side up, on rack in roasting pan. Do not add water; cover pan with lid or cover tightly with foil. Roast 11- to 12-pound turkey for 3 hours. Remove cover and cut band of skin or cord. Baste turkey with pan juices and roast, uncovered, till done, about 1 hour more. The turkey will not be as attractive as in uncovered method. If a covered dark-colored roasting pan is used, the total roasting time will be shorter. Roasting time depends on the size and conformation of the bird. The meat thermometer gives a guide to doneness (185 degrees).

To Roast in Cooking Bags or Wrap

Preheat oven according to manufacturer's direction. Prepare bird as above and insert meat thermometer. Be sure to coat bag or wrap with at least 1 T. flour in order to prevent bursting and release of hot fats and juices. Manufacturers also recommend that holes be punctured in the top of bags as a safety precaution. Use a pan large enough to hold the entire contents of bag or wrap, and deep enough to collect any juices released during roasting. The pan will need to be at least 1 ½ to 2 inches deep. Read and follow manufacturer's directions for roasting, but rely on your meat thermometer for accuracy of doneness.

For Rare Occasions with Beef and Steak

PEPPER STEAK
1   (1-lb.) chuck steak, cut into thin strips
¼ cup salad oil
1   clove garlic, minced
1   T. soy sauce·
1   tsp. salt
1 ¼ cups water, divided
1   cup chopped green pepper
1   cup chopped onion
½ cup chopped celery
2   to 3 T. cornstarch
2   tomatoes, cut in wedges
Hot cooked rice.

Brown steak in hot oil; add garlic and cook about 3 minutes. Add soy sauce, salt, and ¼ cup water; cover and cook 45 minutes. Add all vegetables, except tomatoes, and cook 10 minutes.

Combine cornstarch and 1 cup water; stir into steak mixture. Cook until slightly thick. Add tomatoes, and cook 5 additional minutes. Serve over rice. Yields 6 servings.

Hamburger and Frank Dishes, etc.

HAMBURGER CABBAGE ROLLS
1 cabbage
Mix:
1 pound ground meat
1 egg
1 onion
1 small pepper
Onion tops, parsley, garlic powder, salt, pepper
1 cup rice

Roll in cabbage leaf. Pour 1 can of tomatoes (whole) and 1 can of tomato sauce (water used as needed) over the cabbage rolls. Sprinkle chili powder on top. Cook on medium low heat for 2 hours.

BURGER BASTE

Helps dress-up thrifty burgers, franks, chicken. Combine 1 (6-oz.) can Hunt's Tomato Paste, 1 cup water, ½ cup bottled steak sauce, ⅓ cup lemon juice, ⅓ cup brown sugar, ¼ cup Wesson Oil, ¼ cup minced onion. Simmer 15 minutes. Makes 2½ cups of variety BBQ sauce.

LIVER IN SAUCE

Cut 1 pound liver into strips. Season ¼ cup flour with salt and pepper. Roll liver strips in mixture. Brown liver in heavy fry pan with 3 T. fat. Blend the following for 15 seconds:

1   small coarsely diced onion
2   cups solid pack tomatoes
½   diced, green pepper
Dash cloves
1   T. flour

Pour the blended mixture into the sauce pan over the liver. Cook without cover until sauce thickens slightly. Serves 4.

Fish: Good 'n Cheap

Since fresh fish spoils easily unless handled with care, it should be the last item bought on a list and the first item stored. When fish comes from the market, it should be wrapped in moisture-proof paper, or placed in a covered refrigerator dish, so that the odor does not penetrate other foods. It should be cooked on the same day it is bought.

If it is to be kept longer, it should be frozen hard in a home freezer cabinet or in the freezer compartment of the refrigerator, with wax paper placed between fish fillets before freezing.

To tell *fresh* fish, check the eyes. "Buy the fish that is looking at you," is the way it is sometimes put—to see they are bright, clear, full and moist. The flesh should be elastic, firm and moist, and it should not hold the impression made by a fingernail. The gills should be red and fresh in color, not grayish.

The scales should cling tightly, the color should be lively and unfaded and the odor should be fresh and fishy, not stale and overstrong. Frozen fish should be stored in the refrigerator freezing compartment or home freezer cabinet.

Fish bought "at the dock" or in a fish store is generally cheaper and certainly fresher than fish bought in a supermarket. (You may have a fish store in your community, but don't know it. Check *Yellow Pages.*)

Lacking the cholesterol of beef (which adds sludge to bloodstream) and lacking beef's UP-UP-UP prices, fish is becoming more attractive as THE meat dish on the dinner table.

BAKED COD (works well with Haddock, too)
1 lb. frozen cod
1 tsp. salt
Dash pepper
¼ tsp. paprika
½ cup thinly sliced onion
¾ to 1 cup milk or light cream

Place fish in shallow, foil-lined baking dish; sprinkle with seasonings. Arrange onion rings over top of fish and pour cream over all. Bake uncovered in moderate oven (350°) about 45 minutes. Makes 4 servings. (*Fresh* cod/haddock requires same amount of baking time.)

Eggs for Lunch and Other Times

TANGY POTATOES AND EGGS
1½ pounds potatoes, cooked and cooled
½ cup shortening
1 small onion, chopped
Salt
⅛ tsp. pepper
8 eggs
⅓ cup milk
1 can (1-lb.) stewed tomatoes

Peel potatoes if desired; dice. Heat shortening in 10-inch skillet. Add potatoes, onion, ¾ tsp. salt and the pepper; fry over medium high heat until golden brown, turning potatoes occasionally. Lower heat. Beat eggs with milk and ½ tsp. salt; pour over potatoes and mix lightly. Cover and cook over low heat, without stirring, 12 to 15 minutes, or until omelet is set.

Vegetables

Learning to Love Vegetables

Vegetables—fresh, canned and frozen—are a prime source of certain vitamins and minerals and of important roughage. Dark-green leafy vegetables and deep-yellow ones (kale, chard, collard, mustard and turnip greens, broccoli, carrots, sweet potatoes, yams, ripe tomatoes and winter squash) are rich sources of vitamin A. Vitamin A is not easily destroyed in cooking and in fact is easier for the body to use from cooked vegetables than from raw.

Raw or lightly cooked cabbage, green peppers and dark, leafy greens are excellent sources of vitamin C; potatoes cooked in their skins are a good source too. Vitamin C content is diminished when vegetables are stored too long. To save nutrients, keep these facts in mind:

1. Once vegetables have been harvested, there is a small but steady loss of both flavor and nutrients. This loss is slowed by proper storage (including refrigeration where desirable) and is much slower in root vegetables such as potatoes and carrots than it is in greens. Use highly perishable vegetables (green beans, green peas, asparagus, leafy greens) as soon as possible.

2. Peel and cut up vegetables close to cooking time. If you cut them up sooner, cover and refrigerate.

3. Wash vegetables quickly, and preferably shortly before cooking. Do not soak cut vegetables in water.

4. Cook vegetables (except when stir-frying) in a covered pot, preferably not glass. Use as little water as necessary.

5. Certain nutrients are just under the skin of vegetables. Cook appropriate vegetables, such as potatoes, in their skins and peel after cooking.

6. Do not add baking soda to vegetables to improve color; it destroys some of the nutrients.

7. Cook vegetables for the shortest time necessary. Learn to taste-test vegetables. Cook most vegetables until they are just tender but still crisp and slightly crunchy. Green peas, beets, sweet potatoes and white potatoes, turnips and rutabagas taste best when cooked until soft.

8. If you cook green vegetables for too long at too high a temperature, you will have discolored, unpleasantly flavored vegetables and a kitchen filled with "cabbage" odors.

Learning the Value of Vegetables

Steaming. Steaming vegetables really brings out their subtle flavors and reduces nutrient loss to a minimum. Buy a steamer basket, the kind with a rigid base, three short legs and flexible sides so the basket can be used in pots of different dimensions. Steamer baskets are available in hardware, variety or kitchen-supply stores, but if you don't have one, you can improvise by placing a colander in a pot that fits it and covering the pot with a tight-fitting lid.

To steam vegetables, wash or scrub them, peel if you wish, slice or leave whole. Bring about 1 inch of water to a boil in a pot—just enough to almost touch the base of the steamer. Put the steamer basket in the pot and add the vegetables. Cover pot and let water boil over moderately high heat so vegetables cook in steam. Cooking times vary, but pieces of vegetable 1 inch thick will take about 10 minutes; whole potatoes or beets, 25 to 40 minutes, depending on size. (When cooking time is long, check water level; add more if needed.) Test small pieces of vegetable for doneness by eating a piece; pierce whole roots with a small knife. Remove cooked vegetables from steamer, put them into a serving dish, add butter or margarine, salt and pepper and serve.

Skillet steaming is another excellent, quick way to cook vegetables and requires nothing more than a heavy skillet with a tight-fitting lid. Wash vegetables quickly and peel if necessary. Leave whole or cut into uniform pieces. Bring about ½ inch of water to a boil in a skillet; add vegetables; stir for a few seconds so they heat evenly; then cover and cook over high heat until steam builds up under the lid. Lower heat to moderate and cook vegetables until tender. Carrot slices and leafy greens will take from 5 to 8 minutes; large cubes of beets or sweet potatoes, 10 to 20 minutes, depending on size and desired tenderness.

To avoid scorching, check vegetables once or twice during cooking period to make sure water has not evaporated. When vegetables are tender, drain off any remaining liquid (or serve it with the vegetables), add butter or margarine, salt and pepper or desired seasoning and serve. Omit butter if a sauce is served with vegetables.

Stir-frying is the way Oriental cooks produce those shiny crisp vegetables so beautiful to look at and good to eat. This method is especially suited to tender vegetables like zucchini, but almost any vegetable can be stir-fried if sliced thin enough, if the pan is very hot and if the vegetables are not too crowded. Wash the vegetables and peel if necessary; cut into uniform pieces, ¼ to ½ inch thick. Heat 1 to 2 tablespoons of oil per pound of vegetables in a large heavy skillet or wok. If desired add a little minced garlic or ginger root to the hot oil, and about 10 seconds later stir in the vegetables. Continue cooking, stirring constantly, until vegetables are crisp-tender, about 4 to 6 minutes. Serve hot.

Braising. Vegetables are cooked in a little oil with little or no water added in a covered pot. Use this method for leafy greens (turnip, kale, broccoli) and other relatively tender vegetables; it requires care and careful adjustment of the heat so the vegetables cook but do not scorch.

Wash the vegetables, peel if necessary and cut into uniform, thin slices about ¼ to ½ inch thick; leaves can be shredded or left whole. Heat about 1 tablespoon of oil per pound of vegetables in a medium-sized skillet. Add vegetables to hot oil and stir for a minute or so to heat them evenly. Cover pan, and when steam forms inside, turn heat down to low and cook until vegetables are crisp-tender, about 5 to 10 minutes. Green leaves generally require no more liquid than that which clings to the leaves after washing; hard vegetables such as carrots may require the addition of a tablespoon or two. When vegetables are crisp-tender, add salt and pepper or desired seasoning and serve.

Boiling. As a general, everyday method of cooking vegetables, forget boiling in a large amount of water; too many nutrients get lost in the water and it's too easy to overcook.

Mature roots like potatoes or beets can be steamed or boiled. Place them, unpeeled, in a pot of cold water and bring rapidly to a boil. When vegetables are boiling, turn down the heat, cover the pot and cook until vegetables are tender when pierced with a small knife. Large potatoes and beets may take 30 to 40 minutes.

Beets

Choose smooth, firm beets with a good, deep-red color. If beet greens are still attached, cut them off about 2 inches above the beet as soon as you can, and if they are young and fresh, cook them as you would cook any fresh greens or add them to a salad. Wrapped in plastic, beets will keep a week or more in the refrigerator. One pound serves 2. Wash beets before cooking but do not remove roots or the red color will run into the water. Steam or boil beets with skins on; peel and slice before seasoning and serving. Beets are good sliced, mixed with onion rings and oil and vinegar dressing and served ice-cold. Beets also can be peeled and cubed or shredded and cooked in a very small amount of liquid.

Broccoli

Buy fresh-smelling, firm, dark-green bunches of broccoli with tightly closed bud clusters and no tiny yellow flowers visible. Store in refrigerator wrapped in plastic and use within 5 days. One bunch (1½ to 2 lbs.) serves 4. To prepare for cooking, cut off and discard about 2 inches from the bottom of each stalk, and any large leaves. Cut off and separate the flowerets; cut large stalks either into ½ inch long pieces or into spears; wash quickly. Steamed or skillet-steamed and seasoned with butter, salt and pepper, broccoli is delicious with almost any dish.

Cabbage

Three types of cabbage are common in the United States: smooth-leaved green cabbage, crinkly leaved savoy and deep-purple "red" cabbage. Use smooth-leaved cabbage for slaw or cooking; savoy is best braised. Red cabbage can be used raw or cooked, but avoid using it for a New England boiled dinner unless you want purple broth and anemic cabbage. Choose firm, heavy heads of red or green cabbage with fresh outer leaves. Savoy cabbage is loose-leaved and rarely feels heavy. Uncut and wrapped well, fresh cabbage will keep several weeks in the refrigerator. One pound serves 3 or 4. To prepare for cooking, discard any damaged outer leaves and rinse the cabbage. Shred the cabbage, or cut it into wedges or 1-inch-wide strips. Cabbage is best skillet-steamed or braised. *Watch the pot. Do not overcook.* Cabbage cooks very quickly and is delicious at the crisp-tender stage and a disaster one minute later.

Cauliflower

Choose crisp, firm, heavy heads of cauliflower with creamy white flowerets free of brown blotches. (Occasionally cauliflower with green flowerets can be found in some markets and is good too.) Wrapped well, cauliflower can be stored up to 1 week in the refrigerator. One medium cauliflower (about 1½ lbs.) serves 4. To prepare for cooking, remove the outer stalk leaves and cut out as much of the core as you can (this can be grated and added to coleslaw). Leave the cauliflower whole or break off the flowerets. Cauliflower may be steamed or skillet-steamed. If water is hard, add a few drops of lemon juice or vinegar to prevent discoloration.

Beans (green, snap, pole, wax or string)

Buy bright-green, blemish-free green beans. Wax beans

should be a pale, almost translucent yellow. To test beans for youth, hold a pod next to your ear and squeeze one of the beans inside; bean should burst with a crisp pop. Beans can be stored, wrapped in plastic, for up to 3 days in the refrigerator. To prepare for cooking, wash them quickly and then, as most beans are bred stringless, just cut off both ends.

Beans are delicious whole or cut in 1-inch pieces, steamed or skillet-steamed and served with butter, salt and pepper.

Dried beans and peas are often used as meat substitutes, since they are a rich source of protein. Besides being wholesome and economical, they can be used in a variety of dishes.

Here are some general rules that apply to the preparation of fried beans and peas:

(1) Dried beans and peas soaked in water (usually overnight) before cooking generally look better and have a better flavor. If this water is drained off, add it to soup.

(2) Use about 3 cups water to soak 1 cup dried beans or peas. You can expect 1 cup of these dried vegetables to yield 2½ cups when cooked; 1 pound will yield about 6 cups, or about 8 servings.

(3) A speedy method for soaking is to bring water to a boil in a heavy saucepan, add washed beans, and boil for 2 minutes. Cover; remove from heat, and let stand for 1 hour. Cook as usual. This method is equivalent to soaking for 12 hours in cold water.

Greens

The greens group includes Swiss chard, kale, collard, dandelion and mustard greens. These dark-green leafy vegetables are a specially rich source of vitamin A and should be served often, though dandelion greens are bitter and require an acquired taste. Swiss chard is mild and its tender white stalks are as delicious as the leaves.

Buy fresh-looking greens with deep-green, undamaged leaves. Two pounds serves 4. Greens should be cooked as soon after purchase as possible, but if they must be kept a day or two, store them wrapped in plastic in the refrigerator without washing. Shortly before cooking trim tough ribs and stems, and wash the greens thoroughly several times in tepid water to remove all sand and soil. Greens are best steamed or skillet-steamed in just the water that clings to the leaves; they are good stir-fried too or braised with salt pork. Cooking time for skillet-steaming is 5 to 20 minutes, depending on tenderness of leaves. Take care not to overcook.

Okra

Peak season for okra is July through October. Choose fresh green pods from 2 to 4 inches long—the smaller the better. Avoid pods that look dull, shriveled or blemished. Okra may be left in a brown paper bag and stored in the refrigerator up to one week. One pound serves 4. To prepare okra for cooking, wash pods quickly and trim stem ends if they seem woody. Cook okra whole or sliced. To avoid the mucilaginous quality which is characteristic of moist-cooked okra, stir-fry it, batter dip and deep fry it.

Green Peas

Choose well-filled, bright-green pods that squeak when rubbed between two fingers. If pods seem to be bursting at the seams, peas are too mature. Peas are sweetest when eaten as close to picking as possible, so wrap and refrigerate them and use the same day if possible. Shell peas before cooking; two pounds yield about 2 cups shelled, and serves 4. Peas are good steamed or cooked in a pan with very little water. They also make an elegant puree.

Corn on the Cob

Thanks to refrigerated transportation, good corn is now available almost year round. Yet it is still at its very best when eaten as soon as possible after picking. Corn connoisseurs like to have the water boiling *before* harvesting the corn! Choose full ears of corn with fresh, moist-looking husks and fat, milky kernels that spurt milk when pressed. Corn that has been husked wholly or partly before it is sold is simply not corn at its best. Plan to eat corn the day you buy it, but if it must be stored *leave the husks on,* wrap it in plastic or damp paper towels and refrigerate.

Corn can be steamed or boiled. Pull off outer husk, rub off the corn silk and drop the corn into a large pot of boiling water or place it in a steamer basket over boiling water. Cook 3 to 7 minutes (allow longer time for mature corn). Drain, serve with melted butter or margarine, salt and pepper.

Eggplant

Eggplant comes in several colors—the familiar deep purple, lavender-striped white and a beautiful egglike white favored by Orientals. Most commonly available is the deep-purple eggplant; pick a heavy, firm, shiny one with a fresh green cap. Refrigerate eggplant until needed and plan to use within 4 days, though it will keep longer. One medium eggplant (about 1 ½ lbs.) serves 4. A few eggplant recipes call for preliminary peeling, slicing and salting to remove excess liquid, but this is rarely necessary; just wipe the eggplant with a clean damp cloth. Its mild flavor adapts to many seasonings.

Potatoes and Such

A good way to prepare potatoes is to bake them. Since the nutritional value is high, there is no preparation expense to speak of and they are desirable for leftovers. Always bake at least two more than you need for use in other recipes.

For a different taste in baked potatoes, try paring them, rinsing, drying, brushing with melted margarine or bacon fat, then baking as usual.

Or mash potatoes with salt, pepper, milk and ½ cup sliced celery sauteed in melted fat until just barely tender.

Slice raw potatoes thinly. Fry in heavy skillet over medium heat until tender. Remove from skillet and keep hot. In skillet, make about 1 ½ cups thin white sauce. Season with ½ teaspoon pepper, 1 teaspoon salt and ¼ teaspoon sweet basil. Add fried potatoes gently; reheat briefly.

Instead of mashed potatoes with gravy or sauce, try an Italian-style dish called polenta: Dice fine or chop about 3 medium potatoes. Put in deep heavy kettle with about 1 quart water and 2 teaspoons salt. Stir in ¾ cup cornmeal and bring to boil. Cook, covered, over low heat, stirring frequently, about 45 minutes. Turn onto buttered platter and serve instead of potatoes, rice or noodles.

Speaking of noodles, make your own for a fraction of the cost and greatly superior flavor. You can make a "carload" and store them in a large jar with a tight-fitting lid for a long time. In large bowl, beat 1 egg slightly. Add enough flour to make a very stiff dough. Knead a few times, toss on a slightly floured board and roll paper thin. Roll up like jelly roll. Cut with sharp knife in

⅛″ or ¼″ strips. Separate well. Dry out on the board. Store in covered jar until needed.

Potatoes, White: Choose firm, smooth, clean, well-shaped potatoes with no sign of discoloration and few blemishes. Do not use potatoes that have patches of green. "Idaho" potatoes cook dry and fluffy; they are especially good for baking and frying. Use "new" potatoes with their waxy texture for eating boiled or, because they hold together well, potato salads. "All-purpose" potatoes can be boiled, steamed, scalloped, mashed, baked or fried. Store potatoes in a cool, dark, dry place. Use new potatoes within two weeks. To preserve nutrients scrub potatoes and steam, bake or boil in their skins.

Potatoes, Sweet: Sweet potatoes and yams are interchangeable in recipes, although they do differ slightly. Sweet potatoes have pale golden skins and yellow flesh that is deliciously dry and mealy when cooked. Yams have pale to reddish skins, orange flesh and are moister when cooked. Choose them bright, firm, smooth-skinned and as blemish-free as possible. Sweet potatoes and yams are much more perishable than white potatoes when stored under household conditions. Put them in a cool, dry, dark place and plan to use within 4 or 5 days. Allow one medium-sized sweet potato or yam per serving or half a large one; scrub well, or wash and peel before cooking. Sweet potatoes are delicious baked and served with salt, pepper, and butter.

Preserving Potatoes: If potatoes do begin to form "eyes," they can easily be salvaged. Heloise, a consumer food advisor with King Features, gives this advice:

> First, as soon as I see any eyes, or growth forming on the potatoes, I pick 'em off. This helps and also keeps the potatoes from going pithy for a while.
>
> I immediately bake 'em thoroughly in my oven *without* foil. I let them cool to the touch.
>
> Cut each one in half, scoop out the centers with a spoon, place in mixing bowl and mash while *dry*. I use my beater for this but a potato masher will do.
>
> I then add a *little* water (NOT milk because we are going to freeze 'em) along with a drop or two of yellow food coloring and some oleo. I add salt and ground black pepper, and now is where we start. . . . I grate some cheese on the largest part of my grater (I use lots of cheese) and some raw onions.
>
> I dump this in the mashed potatoes and stir well with fork.

Do NOT heat or use mixer or masher for this.

I fill each baked potato half shell with this goop and then freeze them.

I usually put the potatoes in a throw-away pan, cover with plastic (so I can see), and secure with a few rubber bands.

Next time I want potatoes for supper, it's a lulu just to let them thaw and rebake until thoroughly warm.

I also found that after rebaking the potatoes, and just before removing them from the oven, that if I sprinkle some Parmesan cheese (or any kind of cheese) over the top and let it melt slightly to a brown tinge, that we are back up on cloud nine again.

I call these Peking Potatoes as, when I lived in China, I learned this is the way the Chinese utilize pithy potatoes.

And if you are a garlic lover, either garlic juice or garlic salt may be added to the potato mixture before filling the shell, or it can be sprinkled on top before reheating the potatoes.

For variety, sometimes I add chopped chives, the sliced tops of little green onions or chopped pimentos. Wonderful for color and taste.

Sauerkraut

The folklore of the Pennsylvania Dutch has it that for good things to happen during the year, sauerkraut must be on the New Year's Day dinner table.

Sauerkraut is, simply, brined, fermented cabbage. You might say it's in the pickle family of foods. And, although we may associate it only with German origins, it was supposedly discovered by the Chinese in the third century B.C.

Sauerkraut is a good buy—it's nutritious, and low in calories too. Three-quarters of a cup of kraut provides about one-fourth of the vitamin C needed each day by adults. It's also a good source of calcium and phosphorous. And one cup of undrained sauerkraut contains only 33 calories.

According to the U.S. Department of Agriculture's Agricultural Marketing Service; good quality sauerkraut has a pleasant, characteristic, tart, and tangy flavor. It is crisp and firm in texture, creamy white in color, and free from specks and core material.

It is available canned and in refrigerated packages which come in different sizes to suit all sizes of families. In some areas, there is also a semi-fresh product sold from barrels or similar containers.

But before you rush out to buy your good-luck sauerkraut, decide how you're going to serve it. Either use sauerkraut as it comes from the can or package or simmer it with diced apples or onions—or both—and add brown sugar to taste. Or, serve a cold sauerkraut salad.

Sauerkraut is a natural with pork and pork products so you can use your ingenuity here, too. Cook the sauerkraut with hot dogs, pork roasts, pork chops, pork steaks, spare ribs, or ham and serve this taste combination with mashed potatoes for a hearty New Year's meal.

Or, if you prefer sandwiches, make a Reuben variation with pork sausage patties, sauerkraut, Swiss cheese, and Thousand Island dressing (if desired) on pieces of toasted rye bread.

Spinach

Choose spinach with fresh, bright-green, crisp-looking leaves. Wrap loosely in plastic and refrigerate until needed. For best flavor use within a day or two. Two pounds of spinach serves 4. To prepare for cooking, cut off roots and trim any heavy midribs on leaves. Wash leaves thoroughly in several changes of tepid water to remove all sand. Spinach is delicious steamed 5 to 7 minutes in a covered pot with just the water that clings to the leaves.

Squash, Summer

Summer squash are harvested while still immature, soft-skinned and relatively small. The most common varieties are yellow crookneck, yellow straight neck, zucchini and scallop or pattypan. Choose firm, fresh-looking squash with glossy skin. Store in refrigerator up to 2 weeks; 1 pound serves 3 or 4. To prepare for cooking, wash squash but do not peel. They can be cooked whole, sliced in rounds or strips or grated, and are good steamed, sauteed, stir-fried, broiled or baked.

Cooking with Vegetables

Beans

You can take hours or minutes in the preparation of a bean dish, but both methods can produce equally delicious results.

Starting with dried pea or navy beans, New England Baked Beans are just the dish when you can get it started early in the morning and be around during the day if they need attention during their long oven baking.

If time is short start with canned baked beans and add a few embellishments. In just 10 minutes of skillet cooking you have a tasty dish.

OLD-FASHIONED BAKED BEANS
3   cups dried navy beans (1 ½ lbs.)
¾   pound salt pork
1   medium onion
2   tsp. salt.
¼   cup light-brown sugar, packed
2   tsp. dry mustard
1   cup light molasses

Wash beans, discarding imperfect ones. Cover beans with 2 quarts cold water; refrigerate, covered, overnight. Next day, drain beans. Turn into 6-quart kettle; cover with 2 quarts cold water. Bring to boiling; reduce heat; simmer, covered, 30 minutes. Drain, reserving liquid. Preheat oven to 300 degrees. Trim rind from salt pork. Cut pork almost through, at half-inch intervals. Place onion in bottom of 4-quart bean pot or casserole. Add beans; bury salt pork, cut side down, in center of beans. Heat reserved bean liquid to boiling. Mix remaining ingredients. Stir in 1 cup boiling bean liquid. Pour over beans. Add boiling liquid just to cover beans (about 1 ½ cups).

Carrots

SWEET-SOUR CARROTS
5   cups sliced carrots
1   (10-¾-oz.) can cream of
    tomato soup, undiluted
½   cup salad oil
1   cup sugar
¾   cup vinegar
1   T. prepared mustard
1   medium onion, chopped
1   medium green pepper, chopped
Dash Worcestershire sauce

Cook carrots in salted water until tender; drain and set aside. Combine remaining ingredients, and cook until onion and pepper are tender; add carrots. Place in a covered dish or jar and chill overnight. Yields 10 servings.

Okra

BEEF AND OKRA CASSEROLE
1 pound lean beef, cubed
½ cup chopped onion
¼ cup salad oil
2 T. all-purpose flour
½ cup beef broth or canned bouillon
1 cup water
½ cup chopped green pepper
2 cups sliced carrots
2 cups sliced okra
1 tsp. salt
Dash pepper
1 tsp. Worcestershire sauce

Saute beef and onion in oil until brown; cook slowly, stirring frequently. Blend in flour; add beef broth and water, stirring until mixture thickens. Add remaining ingredients. Cover and simmer about 1 hour, stirring frequently. Yields 6 servings.

Tomatoes

TOMATO GRAVY
6 to 8 medium tomatoes, peeled
1 T. sugar
¾ tsp. salt

Cut tomatoes into quarters; put in a saucepan, and bring to a boil. Remove from heat; put through a food mill, or blend well in an electric blender. Add sugar and salt. Return mixture to saucepan, and simmer until thick. Serve over dried peas or beans. Yields 6 servings.

Good Fritters

VEGETABLE FRITTERS
You can make fritters out of practically any cooked vegetable. Green beans, wax beans, carrots and summer squash are very good; sliced tomatoes are marvelous; even turnips are good. Drain the vegetable. Make a batter out of 1 egg, slightly beaten, ⅔ cup milk, 1 T. oil or melted lard, 1 cup flour and 1 tsp. salt. (For a thinner batter, use 1 cup milk.) Dip vegetable in batter and fry in hot fat until lightly browned (about 3 minutes). Drain and serve.

An Assortment of Vegetables

CORN PUDDING
2   cans creamed corn
Salt and pepper
1   T. sugar
3   T. milk
4   egg yolks

Combine above in large bowl. Then beat 4 egg whites until stiff. Fold together. Preheat oven, 325 degrees. Bake 1 hour 20 minutes.

SQUASH CASSEROLE
4   or 5 large squash
1   medium onion, chopped
2   T. butter
1   tsp. salt
Dash nutmeg and black pepper
Parsley flakes

Steam squash and onion until tender, drain, add butter, nutmeg and parsley. Top with melted cheese and bread crumbs.

Salads, Soups, Stews, Chilis

Jello Salad

ORANGE REFRIGERATOR SALAD
1   (3-oz.) package orange-flavored gelatin
1   (12-oz.) carton small-curd cottage cheese
1   (11-oz.) can mandarin orange sections, drained
1   (8¼-oz.) can crushed pineapple, drained
1   (4½-oz.) carton frozen whipped topping, thawed

Sprinkle dry gelatin over cottage cheese. Add mandarin oranges and pineapple; stir gently to mix well. Fold in whipped topping. Cover and refrigerate for at least 4 hours. Yields 8 to 10 servings.

Vegetable Salad

GREEN BEAN SALAD
1   can sliced green beans (I like the seasoned kind), drained
2   hard-boiled eggs
5   slices crisp bacon, crumbled
1   small onion, chopped
Stalk of celery, chopped

Mix together with salad dressing to taste. Serves 6-8.

Fruit Salad

MACARONI FRUIT SALAD

4   oz. (1 cup) ring macaroni
Salt
Dressing
¾ cup heavy cream
½ tsp. vanilla extract
1   can (11 oz.) mandarin oranges, drained
1 ½ cups seedless green grapes
1   can (8 ½ oz.) pineapple tidbits, drained
½ cup miniature marshmallows

Cook macaroni in boiling salted water until tender. Drain and rinse
with cold water; drain again. Prepare dressing, cover and cool. When
ready to serve, whip cream until almost thick. Add vanilla and beat until
stiff. Fold into dressing. Combine macaroni, fruits and marshmallows.
Add dressing mixture and toss lightly but thoroughly. Makes 6 to 8
servings.

Dressing: In top part of double boiler, combine 2 egg yolks, ¼ cup
light cream, 2 T. sugar and 1 ½ T. lemon juice. Put over simmering
water; cook, stirring, until thick.

Meat or Fish in Your Salad

TUNA WITH PEA SALAD

1   (20-oz.) can chick-peas, drained and rinsed
⅔ cup finely chopped, peeled onion
⅓ cup sliced pitted ripe olives
1   (7-oz.) can solid-packed tuna, drained and broken into large chunks
2   tsp. crushed dried basil leaves
1   T. dried parsley flakes
½ cup olive or vegetable oil
1   tsp. dry mustard
½ tsp. salt
⅛ tsp. pepper
2 cloves garlic, peeled and minced

In a medium-sized bowl place chick-peas, onion, olives, tuna, basil and
parsley. Measure oil in a 1-cup measuring cup; add remaining ingredients and mix well. Pour dressing over chick-pea mixture and toss
gently. Serve at once or chill 10 minutes in the freezer or slightly longer
in the refrigerator. Makes about 3 ½ cups, or 4 servings.

Your time: 16 minutes. Chilling time (optional): 10 minutes.

Soup and Chowder

Soup

CREAM SOUPS

(Good for left-over vegetables)
Blend for 1 minute:
3 T. flour
1 tsp. salt
3 T. butter
2 tsp. Worcestershire sauce
1 ½ cups milk

Pour into saucepan and cook slowly. Stir until sauce thickens. Place in blender and blend until smooth. 1 cup sliced cooked vegetables, 1 ½ cups bouillon, vegetable or meat stock, or broth.

Add contents of blender to saucepan. Simmer until hot. Serves 6.

Chowder

TURKEY CORN CHOWDER

4 slices bacon, cut up
1 cup chopped onion
4 cups (1 ¾ lbs.) cubed, pared potato
2 cups turkey broth
2 packages (10-oz. size) frozen whole-kernel corn, thawed
¼ cup butter or regular margarine
2 ½ tsp. salt
¼ tsp. pepper
2 cups cooked turkey, cut up into large chunks
2 cups milk
1 cup heavy cream
2 T. chopped parsley

In 5-quart Dutch oven or heavy kettle, saute bacon until crisp; remove; reserve.

In bacon fat, saute onion, stirring, until golden—about 5 minutes. Add potato and turkey broth. Bring to boiling; simmer, covered, about 30 minutes, or just until potato is tender but not mushy.

Meanwhile, in medium saucepan, combine corn, butter, salt, pepper, turkey and milk. Simmer, covered and stirring occasionally, 10 minutes.

Add to potato mixture, along with the heavy cream. Cook, stirring occasionally, until hot—do not boil.

Turn into warm soup tureen; sprinkle with reserved crisp bacon and chopped parsley. Serve with chowder crackers. Makes 8 to 10 servings.

Stew

BROWNED BEEF STEW

2 pounds beef (cut in 2-in. cubes)
2 T. fat
2 tsp. salt
¼ tsp. pepper
¼ tsp. thyme
½ tsp. seasoning salt
3 bouillon cubes dissolved in
  3 cups hot water
8 small whole onions
12 small whole potatoes
6 carrots, cut in ½" slices
1 box frozen green peas

Preheat skillet to 325 degrees. Add 2 T. fat and brown beef cubes. Add bouillon, cover and simmer at 200 degrees for about 35 minutes. Thicken with 2 T. flour mixed with ¼ cup water. Add potatoes, carrots and onions and cook for 40 minutes.

Add peas about 5 minutes before stew is to be served. Serves 6 to 8.

Chili

HEARTY CHILI
Serve piping hot with cornbread. Ole!

Brown 1 pound hamburger, 1 cup chopped onion, 1 clove garlic, minced. Drain fat. Stir in 2 (15-oz.) cans small red beans, undrained, 1 (6-oz.) can tomato paste, 1 T. chili powder, 1 tsp. salt. Simmer, uncovered, 30 minutes. 6 servings.

Knowing and Using Spices: The Key to Good Cheap Food

One of the best meals I ever ate was in a tin-roofed hut in a mountaintop construction camp for coolies in Taiwan. The food and spices in that wooden bowl of nuts, cabbage and greens were cheap. But the taste of the mixture I shoved into my mouth with chopsticks was rich and full. The proper blending of spices did it.

Check it out for yourself: the best dishes in French, Italian, Thai, Greek, etc., cuisine acquire their keep-'em-coming-back-for-more tastes not so much from inclusion of esoteric, expensive ingredients but from the proper blending of spices. French soups, Italian pastas, Thai rice dishes, and Greek salads are *par excellence* because of the magic of spices.

You can do it too. Using the following chart*, you can create your own infinitely varied and zesty *good cheap food*.

APPLE PIE SPICE: A blend of spices for apple pie. May be used in other apple dishes, sweet potatoes, squash, sweet breads, French toast, puddings, coffee cakes, custards, steamed puddings or cookies.

ANISE SEED: Characteristic ingredient of Springerle cookies. Also use when preparing baked apples, coffee cake, fruit salads, fruit salad dressings, stewed fruits, cakes, cookies, cream cheese spreads, rolls or baked fish.

ARROWROOT: An excellent thickening agent. Especially good to thicken fruit sauces as it leaves the sauce clear. Arrowroot does not brown; therefore, it is not recommended for use in gravies or brown sauce.

BARBECUE SPICE: A blend of spices with slight "smoky" flavor. Use when preparing beef, pork, lamb, veal, baked beans, tomatoes, eggplant, peas, potatoes, onions, chicken, fish, shrimp, seasoned butters, barbecue sauce or spaghetti sauce. Excellent to use in both indoor and outdoor cooking.

BEEF FLAVOR BASE AND CHICKEN SEASONED STOCK BASE: Two all-purpose seasonings. Add rich flavor to soups, stews, gravies, pot pies, vegetables, sauces, rice, noodles, stuffings, casseroles and some salads. May also be used to make stock or broth.

BELL PEPPER FLAKES: Adds flavor and color to vegetable soup, minestrone, Manhattan clam chowder, gumbos, stews, pot roasts, pot pies, chicken casseroles, Spanish rice, stewed tomatoes, tomato sauces or spaghetti sauce.

CINNAMON SUGAR: A perfect blend of ground cinnamon and sugar used in making cinnamon toast. Use also to sprinkle over coffee cakes, cup cakes, cookies, baked apples, stewed fruit, French toast, pancakes or waffles.

CORIANDER SEED: Use whole in pickles, soups, punch or

---

*Courtesy of McCormick & Co., Inc., Baltimore, Md.

marinades. Crush the seed and use in preparing cakes, cookies, gingerbread, fruit pies, apple dishes, chicken, fish, seasoned butter, pork, biscuits, corn bread, steamed puddings, Danish pastry, hamburgers, meat pies or stuffings.

CREAM OF TARTAR: A chemical rather than a spice. Used extensively in dishes using beaten egg whites such as angel food cake, meringue shells, meringues for pies, 7-minute frosting or cakes calling for beaten egg whites. Also may be used in biscuits of fondants. Removes stains from aluminum cooking utensils.

CUMIN: Use whole or ground in meat loaf, hamburgers, pot roast, stews, lentil soup, pea soup, tomato sauces, egg dishes, rice, salad dressings, game, Mexican-style dishes, dried bean dishes or potato salad.

DILL SEED: Use when preparing dill pickles, Kosher dill pickles, cauliflower, cabbage, sauerkraut, salad dressings, breads, pickled beets, green beans, fish or shellfish. Dill Salt is a blend of ground Dill Seed and salt. Use on tomatoes, potatoes, cauliflower, tossed green salads and some meats.

DILL WEED: A milder dill flavor than Dill Seed. Use when preparing dips, canapés, tossed green salads, salad dressings, tuna salad, potato salad, broiled or baked fish, sautéed shrimp, bread, rice, noodles, stuffed eggs, scrambled eggs, chicken, carrots, potatoes, cauliflower or beets.

FENNEL SEED: An ancient spice used today in preparing fish, spiced shrimp, oyster dishes, artichokes, cauliflower, broccoli, Brussels sprouts, potatoes, potato salad, coffee cakes, apple cakes, baked apples, tomato sauce, spaghetti sauce or breads.

GARLIC: Powder, Salt, Chips, Minced, Liquid and Juice. Use in preparing tossed green salads, salad dressings, beef, lamb, pork, veal, variety meats, game, green beans, tomatoes, eggplant, tomato sauce, spaghetti sauce, Kosher dill pickles, pizza sauce, baked fish, broiled fish, sea food dishes or bread.

GUMBO FILÉ: A thickening agent used in gumbos. Do not heat after Gumbo Filé has been added.

HORSERADISH, POWDERED: A tangy dehydrated form of horseradish. Use in tomato juice, vegetable juice, cream sauce, whipped cream, sour cream, baked beans, ham glazes, dips or liver pâté. Also use when preparing many meat dishes.

ITALIAN SEASONING: A blend of herbs with an Italian accent. May be used when preparing pizza sauce, spaghetti sauce, barbecue sauce, veal Parmesan, lasagne, Italian dressing, minestrone, shrimp and many other Italian dishes.

MEAT TENDERIZER: Available seasoned and non-seasoned. Used to tenderize less tender cuts of meat such as chuck, round steak, stew meat, brisket or flank steak.

MINT FLAKES: Adds the refreshing taste of mint to iced tea, punch, dessert sauces, fruit compotes, custards, ice cream, frostings, chocolate cake, peas or lamb stew. May be used when making mint jelly.

MSG: A chemical rather than a spice. Brings out natural flavor of many foods without imparting flavor of its own. Use when preparing meat, fish, poultry, vegetables, tossed green salads and many sauces.

ONION: Powder, Salt, Flakes, Minces, Chopped, Juice and Shredded Green. A versatile product in many forms. Use in dishes where an onion flavor is desirable. Use Onion Juice in dishes where a mild onion flavor is desired without the particles of onion.

PEPPER, BLACK: Cracked, Coarse Grind, Fine Grind, and Whole or Peppercorns. The universal seasoning. Use when preparing meats, vegetables, soups, most salads, pfeffernusse, spice cake, sea food, cheese dishes, marinades or eggs.

PEPPER, WHITE: Milder in flavor than Black Pepper. Use as Black Pepper—especially in foods where the dark specks of Black Pepper are undesirable.

RED PEPPER, CRUSHED: Hot and tangy. Used especially in pickling and Mexican or Italian dishes. Also use when preparing hamburgers, creole dishes, marinades, spiced shrimp, gumbos, chowders or steamed crabs. Use with care.

SAFFRON: The most expensive of all spices, but a little bit goes a long way. Prized for the golden yellow color it imparts to foods such as bread, cakes, rice, soups and international dishes such as arroz con pollo, paella, risotto or bouillabaisse.

SALAD HERBS: A blend of herbs designed especially for making salads. Sprinkle over tossed green salads before tossing or use in salad dressings.

SAVORY: An herb used when preparing stuffings, herb bread, herb waffles, chicken or turkey dishes, broccoli, green beans, lima beans, Brussels sprouts, tomato soup, vegetable soup, stews or meat pies.

TARRAGON: An excellent herb to use when preparing fish and shellfish. It is the distinctive flavor in Béarnaise sauce. May also be used when preparing marinades, chicken, turkey, game, egg dishes, tossed green salads or salad dressings.

TURMERIC: Adds a bright yellow color to egg dishes, soups, pickles, corn relish, chow-chow, rice, noodles, sauces, chicken, sea food, mayonnaise or salad dressings.

VEGETABLE FLAKES: A blend of dehydrated vegetables. Use in stews, soups, gravies, casseroles, pot roast, meat pies, molded vegetable salads or Spanish omelettes.

	APPETIZERS	SOUPS	SALADS AND SALAD DRESSINGS	VEGETABLES
ALLSPICE	Swedish Meat Balls, Cranberry Relish, Spiced Nuts, Pickled Eggs	Fruit Soup, Asparagus, Cream of Pea, Minestrone, Chicken, Tomato	Tomato Aspic, Fruit Salads, French Dressing, Cottage Cheese	Beets, Sweet Potatoes, Squash Carrots, Eggplant, Spinach, Baked Beans
BASIL LEAVES	Pizza, Butter or Cream Cheese Spreads, Meat Balls, Marinated Mushrooms	Tomato, Vegetable, Lentil, Pea, Minestrone	Tomato Aspic, Tossed Green Salads, Potato, French Dressing, Herb Dressing, Sea Food, Egg	Tomatoes, Peas, Cauliflower, Potatoes Carrots, Spinach, Eggplant, Squash
BAY LEAVES	Tomato Juice, Marinated Fish, Artichokes or Mushrooms	Chicken, Onion, Gumbo, Clam Chowder, Tomato, Vegetable, Lobster Bisque	Sea Food, Tomato Aspic, French Dressing, Herb Dressing	In Water When Cooking Most Vegetab Pickled Beets, Rice
BON APPÉTIT	Cheese Dips, Tomato Juice, Spreads, Liver Pâté, Stuffed Celery	Vegetable, Tomato, Pea, Chicken, Lentil, Clam Chowder, Oyster Stew, Lobster Bisque	Tossed Green Salads, Sea Food, Coleslaw, Potato, Macaroni, Herb or Roquefort Dressing	Peas, Beans, Corn, Potatoes, Eggplant, Rice, Tomatoes, Squash, Turnips
CARAWAY SEED	Dips, Cheese Spreads, Cheese Straws	Borscht, Corn, Pea, Potato, Vegetable	Potato, Coleslaw, Cucumber	Sauerkraut, Cabbage Potatoes, Cauliflower Carrots, Squash, Beets, Beans
CARDAMON SEED	Spiced Nuts, Fruit Cocktail	Green Pea, Fruit Soup	Fruit Salads, Fruit Salad Dressings	Sweet Potatoes, Squash, Rice Baked Beans
CAYENNE or RED PEPPER & CAYENNE	Deviled Eggs, Cheese Straws, Dips, Tomato Juice, Spreads, Guacamole	Oyster Stew, Chowders, Cream Soups, Vegetable Soup, Tomato Soup	Sea Food, Potato, Coleslaw, Macaroni, Cucumber, French Dressing, Kidney Bean	Corn, Onions, Potatoes, Asparagus Broccoli, Eggplant
CELERY Salt, Flakes, Seed	Tomato Juice, Ham Spread, Cheese Spread, Dips, Canapés, Sauerkraut Juice	Cream of Celery, Tomato, Vegetable, Asparagus, Pea, Lentil, Oyster Stew	Tomato Aspic, Potato, Macaroni, Egg. Coleslaw, Dressing for Fruit Salads	Tomatoes, Okra, Broccoli, Sauerkrau Asparagus, Onions, Potatoes, Corn
CHILI POWDER	Guacamole, Cheese Balls, Cheese Dips, Deviled Ham Spread	Tomato, Corn, Pepperpot, Chowders, Pea	Kidney Bean, French Dressing, Mayonnaise or Sour Cream Dressing	Corn, Eggplant, Tomatoes, Carrots, Rice, Baked Beans, Onions
CINNAMON	Broiled Grapefruit, Spiced Nuts, Cereal Nibblers, Fruit Cocktail	Fruit Soup, Tomato, Vegetable, Chicken	Mixed Fruit Salads, Waldorf Salad, Fruit Salad Dressings	Sweet Potatoes, Squash Spinach, Asparagus, Broiled Bananas, Rice Beets, Carrots
CLOVES	Tomato Juice, Spiced Nuts, Pickled Eggs, Cranberry Relish	Bean, Tomato, Vegetable, Pea, Clam Chowder	Tomato Aspic, Frozen Fruit Salads, Mixed Fruit Salads, Fruit Salad Dressings	Beets, Onions, Squash, Sweet Potatoe Baked Beans, Rice, Tomatoes
CURRY POWDER	Dips, Cheese Spreads, Chicken Balls, Cereal Nibblers, Meat Balls	Mulligatawny, Curry Soup	Sea Food Salads, French Dressing, Mayonnaise or Sour Cream Dressing	Creamed Vegetables Rice
GINGER	Broiled Grapefruit, Beef Teriyaki, Spiced Nuts, Rumaki, Spreads for Fruit or Nut Breads	Chicken, Onion, Carrot, Fish Chowders	Mixed Fruit Salads, Frozen Fruit Salads, Fruit Salad Dressings	Carrots, Squash, Sweet Potato Beets, Baked Beans
HERB SEASONING	Tomato Juice, Dips. Spreads, Cocktail Pizza, Liver Pâté	Tomato, Vegetable, Lentil, Chowders, Bean, Potato	Potato, Coleslaw, Tomato Aspic, French Dressing, Herb Dressing	Eggplant, Tomatoes Lima Beans, Brocco Scalloped Potatoes, Mushrooms

EGGS AND CHEESE	MEATS AND MEAT SAUCES	POULTRY AND FISH	DESSERTS & BAKED GOODS
Pickled Eggs, Cream Cheese Spreads, Spanish Omelettes, French Toast	Pot Roast, Ground Beef, Baked Ham, Stews, Tomato Sauce, Marinades, Barbecue Sauce	Creamed Chicken, Poached Fish, Spiced Shrimp	Mincemeat, Fruit Compotes, Spice Cake, Cookies, Steamed Puddings, Pie Crust, Fruit Pies
Scrambled Eggs, Cheese Spreads	Pork, Beef, Veal, Lamb, Venison, Tomato Sauce, Barbecue Sauce	Duck, Lobster, Shrimp, Chicken, Turkey, Stuffings	Herb Bread, Waffles, Croutons
Eggs Creole, Spanish Omelette, Pickled Eggs	Beef Stew, Pot Roast, Sauerbraten, Lamb Stew, Tomato Sauce, Barbecue Sauce	Stewed Chicken, Spiced Shrimp, Poached Fish, Shrimp Creole	Custard Sauce
Most Egg Dishes, Cheese Soufflé, Fondue, Cheese Sauce	Pork, Beef, Lamb, Veal, Variety Meats, Tomato Sauce, Gravies, Barbecue Sauce	Chicken, Turkey, Duck, Goose, Sea Food, Fish, Cornish Hens, Stuffings	Herb Bread, Waffles
Cottage Cheese, Omelettes, Macaroni and Cheese	Pork, Beef or Lamb Stew, Marinades for Meats	Goose, Duck, Guinea Hen, Tuna Casserole, Stuffings	Rye Bread, Waffles, Corn Bread, Biscuits, Pastry for Meat Pies, Spice Cake, Pound Cake
French Toast	Pot Roast, Pork Roast, Sauerbraten, Barbecue Sauce	Poached Fish	Cakes, Cookies, Puddings, Fruit Compotes, Custard, Danish Pastry, Coffee Cakes, Gingerbread
Cheese Soufflé, Omelettes, Macaroni and Cheese, Creamed Eggs, Welsh Rabbit, Hollandaise Sauce	Pork Chops, Pot Roast, Stews, Barbecue Sauce, Gravies	Chicken Dishes, Crab Cakes, Deviled Crab or Lobster, Turkey Pie	
Stuffed Eggs, Cheese Soufflé, Omelettes, Macaroni and Cheese, Welsh Rabbit	Pot Roast, Meat Loaf, Stews, Sauerbraten, Spiced Tongue, Tomato Sauce, Barbecue Sauce	Goose, Duck, Chicken, Turkey, Cornish Hens, Tuna Casseroles, Broiled Fish, Stuffings	Rolls, Biscuits, Dumplings
Omelettes, Soufflé, Welsh Rabbit, Stuffed Eggs	Meat Loaf, Stews, Venison, Hamburgers, Chili con Carne, Gravies, Pot Roast	Chicken with Rice, Sea Food Casseroles	Croutons
French Toast	Ham, Pork Shoulder, Boiled Beef, Pork Chops, Tomato Sauce, Barbecue Sauce	Poached Fish, Stewed Chicken, Spiced Shrimp	Cookies, Cakes, Custards, Puddings, Coffee Cakes, Stewed or Baked Fruit, Fruit Pies, Rolls, Toast
Cream Cheese Spreads, Deviled Eggs	Ham, Boiled Beef, Sauerbraten, Pork Shoulder, Pork Chops, Tomato and Barbecue Sauces, Sauce for Ham	Chicken Casseroles, Poached Fish, Spiced Shrimp, Crab Cakes, Baked Fish	Cakes, Cookies, Fruit Pies, Pastry, Sweet Rolls, Coffee Cakes, Puddings, Custards, Dessert Sauces
Egg Casseroles, Stuffed Eggs, Curried Eggs, Scrambled Eggs	Lamb, Pork, Beef, Curry Sauces	Shrimp, Lobster, Chicken, Turkey, Oysters	Fruit Compotes, Waffles, Rolls
Macaroni and Cheese, Cheese Soufflé, French Toast	Pork Roast, Pork Chops, Spareribs, Veal, Beef, Venison, Barbecue Sauce, Gravies	Roast Chicken, Chicken Casseroles, Duck, Turkey, Baked Fish, Shellfish	Gingerbread, Cakes, Cookies, Toast, Fruit Compotes, Custards, Puddings, Ice Cream, Dessert Sauces
Stuffed Eggs, Macaroni and Cheese, Omelettes	Beef, Veal, Lamb, Pork, Variety Meats, Game, Gravies, Spaghetti Sauce, Barbecue Sauces	Baked Fish, Broiled Fish, Spiced Shrimp, Crab Cakes, Chicken, Stuffings	Herb Bread, Waffles, Corn Bread, Herb Croutons

LEMON AND ORANGE PEEL	Spiced Nuts, Spreads for Fruit or Nut Breads and Cranberry Relish	Fruit Soup,	Fruit Salad Dressings, Waldorf Salad, Mixed Fruit Salads	Spinach, Carrots, Squash, Sweet Potatoes, Broccoli
MARJORAM	Meat Balls, Dips, Cocktail Pizza, Tomato Juice, Marinated Artichokes or Mushrooms	Onion, Turtle, Tomato, Vegetable, Spinach, Scotch Broth, Minestrone, Mushroom	Tomato Aspic, Tossed Green Salads, Herb Dressing	Carrots, Peas, Beans, Broccoli, Cauliflower, Brussels Sprouts, Spinach, Mushrooms, Zucchini
MUSTARD SEED OR DRY MUSTARD	Meat Balls, Dips, Ham Spreads, Tomato Juice, Pickled Eggs, Cheese Spreads	Tomato, Vegetable, Chowders, Lentil, Chicken, Potato	Coleslaw, Chicken, Potato, Macaroni, Italian Dressing, Lamaze Dressing, Mayonnaise	Asparagus, Corn, Potato, Baked Beans, Onion, Cauliflower
NUTMEG AND MACE	Eggnog, Canapes, Spiced Nuts, Meat Balls, Liver Pate	Chicken, Mushroom, Vegetable, Fruit Soup, Chowders, Oyster Stew, Split Pea, Cream of Spinach	Mixed Fruit Salads, Frozen Fruit Salads, Fruit Salad Dressings, Waldorf Salad	Spinach, Squash, Asparagus, Broccoli, Sweet Potatoes, Carrots, Green Beans
OREGANO	Meat Balls, Dips, Cocktail Pizza, Tomato Juice, Marinated Artichokes	Vegetable, Tomato, Minestrone, Onion, Chowders, Lentil	Tomato Aspic, Egg, Tuna, Salmon, Italian Dressing, Mayonnaise Dressing	Tomatoes, Carrots, Peas, Potatoes, Squash, Spinach, Beans, Turnips, Eggplant
PAPRIKA	Garnish for Canapes, Stuffed Celery, Dips, Cheese Straws	Garnish for Most Soups	Garnish for Tuna, Chicken, Egg, Macaroni or Potato Salads, French Dressing, Mayonnaise	Garnish for Potatoes, Onions, Cauliflower, Carrots, Asparagus, Creamed Vegetables
PARSLEY FLAKES	Cheese Spreads, Dips, Marinated Mushrooms or Artichokes	Garnish for Most Soups	Egg, Tuna, Chicken, Macaroni, Potato, Italian Dressing, Herb Dressing	Potatoes, Carrots, Cauliflower, Onions, Tomatoes, Eggplant, Peas, Rice
PICKLING SPICE	Marinated Mushrooms, Artichokes or Fish, Pickled Cauliflower	Beef Broth, Tomato, Vegetable	Tomato Aspic, Herb Dressing	Pickled Beets
POPPY SEED	Cheese Sticks, Dips, Spreads, Garnish		Mixed Fruit Salads, Fruit Salad Dressings	Potatoes, Noodles, Rice, Sweet Potatoes, Squash, Carrots, Asparagus, Turnips
POULTRY SEASONING	Meat Balls, Chicken Spread, Cheese Balls	Chicken, Minestrone, Lentil, Split Pea, Bean	Chicken, Turkey, SeaFood	Lima Beans, Green Beans, Eggplant, Onions
PUMPKIN PIE SPICE	Spiced Nuts, Spreads for Tea Sandwiches	Fruit Soup	Frozen Fruit Salads, Fruit Salad Dressings	Squash, Sweet Potatoes, Carrots, Rutabagas
ROSEMARY	Liver Pâté, Tomato Juice, Fruit Juice	Vegetable, Tomato, Chicken, Beef Broth, Minestrone, Pea	Tomato Aspic, Sea Food, Herb Dressing	Potatoes, Tomatoes, Cauliflower, Carrots, Lima Beans, Turnips, Green Beans, Zucchini, Brussels Sprouts, Cabbage
SAGE	Meat Balls, Chicken Spread, Cheese Balls	Minestrone, Vegetable, Tomato, Chicken, Chowders	Herb Dressing	Lima Beans, Peas, Onions, Tomatoes, Brussel Sprouts, Eggplant
SEASON-ALL	Tomato Juice, Dips, Spreads, Cheese Straws, Liver Pate, Meat Balls,	Tomato, Vegetable, Corn, Onion, Chicken, Chowders, Bean	Potato, Chicken, Macaroni, Egg, Mayonnaise Dressing	Most Vegetables
SESAME SEED	Cereal Nibblers, Stuffed Mushrooms, Canapes, Cheese Balls		Tossed Green Salads, Fruit Salads, Fruit Salad Dressings	Tomatoes, Vegetable Casseroles, Asparagus, Mushrooms
THYME	Liver Pâté, Cocktail Pizza, Meat Balls, Tomato Juice, Sauerkraut Juice	Vegetable, Tomato, Minestrone, Manhattan Clam Chowder, Chicken Gumbos, Bouillabaisse	Tomato Aspic, Herb Salad Dressing	Tomatoes, Onions, Brussels Sprouts, Broccoli, Lima Beans, Zucchini, Green Beans

Cream Cheese Spreads, French Toast	Marinades, Pork, Veal, Ham, Stuffings, Hamburgers	Sauce for Duck Baked Fish, Broiled Fish, Duck, Chicken, Stuffings	Whipped Cream, Toppings, Dessert Sauces, Toast, Fruit Pies, Pastry, Baked or Stewed Fruit
Scrambled Eggs, Omelettes, Stuffed Eggs, Cheese Sauce, Hollandaise Sauce	Beef, Veal, Pork, Lamb, Variety Meats, Game, Tomato Sauce, Barbecue Sauce	Baked Fish, Broiled Fish, Spiced Shrimp, Crab Cakes, Chicken Dishes, Stuffings	Waffles, Herb Bread, Corn Bread, Croutons
Stuffed Eggs, Omelettes, Cheese Soufflé, Welsh Rabbit, Cheese Sauce, Creamed Eggs	Beef, Veal, Pork, Lamb, Variety Meats, Game, Tomato Sauce, Barbecue Sauce	Chicken, Turkey, Duck, Goose, Cornish Hens, Fish, Sea Food	Biscuits
Cheese Fondue, Cream Cheese Spreads, Soufflés, Creamed Eggs, French Toast, Welsh Rabbit	Hamburgers, Veal, Beef, Pork, Lamb, Gravies, Cream Sauces, Tomato Sauce, Barbecue Sauce	Chicken, Turkey, Cornish Hens, Goose, Duck, Fish, Creamed Sea Food	Doughnuts, Cakes, Cookies, Coffee Cakes, Sweet Breads, Stewed Fruit, Custards, Puddings, Dessert Sauces and Toppings
Stuffed Eggs, Omelettes, Cream Cheese Spreads, Cottage Cheese	Hamburgers, Meat Loaf, Veal, Pork, Lamb, Beef, Game, Tomato Sauce, Spaghetti Sauce	Chicken Dishes, Baked Fish, Broiled Fish, Tuna Casseroles, Stuffings	Herb Bread, Rolls, Waffles, Croutons
Garnish for Egg and Cheese Dishes	Hungarian Goulash, Veal Paprika, Garnish for Meats	Chicken Paprika, Garnish for Poultry and Fish, Excellent Browning Agent for Fried Chicken or Fish	Rolls
Scrambled Eggs, Stuffed Eggs, Omelettes, Cheese Sauces, Creamed Eggs	Pot Roast, Stews, Hamburgers, Meat Loaf, Veal Dishes, Tomato Sauces, Spaghetti Sauce	Chicken Dishes, Broiled Fish, Baked Fish, Spiced Shrimp, Stuffings, Croquettes	Biscuits, Waffles, Rolls, Dumplings
Pickled Eggs	Stews, Pot Roast, Sauerbraten, Spaghetti Sauce, Barbecue Sauce, Beef Brisket, Tongue, Marinades	Stewed Chicken, Boiled Shrimp	Stewed Fruit
Cottage Cheese, Cream Cheese, Scrambled Eggs, Omelettes, Macaroni and Cheese, French Toast	Veal and Sour Cream, Stuffing for Pork Chops	Tuna Casseroles, Chicken Casseroles, Stuffings, Chicken Livers	Danish Pastry, Cakes, Cookies, Breads, Fruit Compotes, Fillings, Dumplings
Omelettes, Scrambled Eggs	Veal Dishes, Gravies, Brown Sauce, Stews, Stuffings for Pork, Lamb or Veal, Croquettes	Chicken, Turkey, Duck, Goose, Stuffings	Waffles, Biscuits, Croutons, Dumplings
French Toast	Orange Sauce for Pork	Sauce for Duck	Pumpkin Pie, Cakes, Cookies, Coffee Cakes, Stewed Fruit, Sweet Breads, Waffles
	Stew, Lamb, Beef, Venison, Spaghetti Sauce, Barbecue Sauce, Pizza Sauce, Veal, Rabbit	Chicken Dishes, Baked Fish, Spiced Shrimp, Stuffings, Poached Fish	Herb Bread, Fruit Compotes, Corn Bread, Dumplings, Biscuits
Egg and Cheese Casseroles, Omelettes, Cheese Sauce	Stews, Pot Roast, Beef, Lamb, Pork, Venison, Gravies, Meat Loaf, Veal	Chicken, Duck, Turkey, Goose, Fish, Stuffings	Waffles, Dumplings
Most Egg and Cheese Dishes	All Meats, Most Sauces	All Poultry, All Fish or Sea Food	Herb Bread, Waffles
Cheese Spreads, Cottage Cheese, Scrambled Eggs	Steaks, Veal Dishes, Stuffings for Pork Chops, Breast of Veal or Crown Roasts	Stuffings, Fried Chicken	Cakes, Cookies, Pastry, Bread, Waffles, Biscuits, Dumplings
Spanish Omelette	Lamb, Beef, Pork, Veal, Game, Variety Meats, Liver, Gravies, Barbecue Sauces, Spaghetti Sauce	Chicken, Turkey, Duck, Goose, Baked or Broiled Fish, Spiced Shrimp, Croquettes, Stuffings	Herb Bread, Dumplings

Breads

James Beard, food expert and gourmet, says:

It is a mysterious business, this making of bread. Once you are hooked by the miracle of yeast, you'll be a bread maker for the rest of your life. . . . If you can read, have an oven and a work space, there is no reason why you can't make a decent loaf of bread.[13]

If you can't you'd better learn. Industry experts, groaning over the massive Russian wheat deals, are predicting bread to shoot to a dollar a loaf! One housewife, intending to fight back, says:

I have carefully calculated that my wholewheat bread costs just about 15 cents a loaf to bake against the 65 cents per loaf for comparable store bought bread. I really start from scratch because I even grind the whole grain wheat into flour to make this bread. For anyone who is looking for a way to save food dollars you can't miss with this recipe.

FOOLPROOF WHOLEWHEAT BREAD
2   T. yeast in ½ cup warm water
5   cups hot water from tap
7   cups unsifted whole wheat flour
⅔   cup honey (or molasses, or ⅓ cup each)
⅔   cup cooking oil
2   T. salt
5   to 6 cups more whole wheat flour

Sprinkle yeast in ½ cup warm water. Do NOT stir. Combine 5 cups hot tap water and 7 cups flour in mixer bowl and mix on LOW speed, while you combine oil, salt and honey (or molasses) in a separate bowl. Add the salt, oil and honey to the mixture in the bread mixer and continue to mix until everything is well blended.

By this time, the yeast should have had plenty of time to brew. The yeast should be on top of the water. Add to ingredients in the mixing bowl and blend thoroughly. Add 5 to 6 cups of flour. Let the dough knead on low speed for 10 minutes in heavy-duty mixer or knead by hand for 10 minutes.

Grease three bread pans. Oil hands and the counter. Remove dough from mixer, ⅓ of the amount at a time. The dough will be sticky, but will easily form into loaves by shaping on the greased counter. Bake at 350 degrees for 40 minutes. When bread has baked, remove immediately from the pans. For a softer crust, brush tops of loaves with oil or butter. Cover with a kitchen towel to cool.

GINGERBREAD

2 cups sifted flour	¼ cup shortening
1 tsp. cinnamon	⅓ cup sugar
¼ tsp. ginger	1 egg
1 tsp. salt	½ cup molasses
½ tsp. nutmeg	½ cup hot water
1½ tsp. baking powder	

Preheat oven to 350 degrees. Grease and flour pan. Sift together flour, cinnamon, ginger, salt, nutmeg and baking powder. Cream shortening and sugar, beat in egg and add molasses. Add dry ingredients alternately with hot water, blending well after each addition. Pour batter into a greased 8-inch square pan. Bake 50-55 minutes or until done. Makes 9 servings.

HEIRLOOM BREAD

2 cups flour	½ cup chopped nuts
1 cup sugar	½ cup raisins
½ cup shortening	1 tsp. soda
2 eggs	1 tsp. baking powder
1 cup applesauce	

Combine and bake at 350 degrees for about 45 minutes.

Rolls

SMALL FAMILY DINNER ROLLS

2 T. soft shortening
1 package dry yeast
1 cup warm water (not hot)
2 T. sugar
1 tsp. salt
2½ cups sifted flour
1 egg
Poppy or sesame seeds (optional)

Dissolve yeast in water. Stir in sugar, salt and ½ the flour. Beat until smooth. Scrape down the sides of bowl. Seal bowl. Let rise in warm place to double size for 45 minutes. Grease muffin tins. Punch down dough. Turn out on pastry sheet. Press dough flat, cut with cutter or shape into clover leafs. Place in tins, let rise again. Brush with melted butter. Sprinkle with seeds. Bake in preheated 400-degree oven 15-20 minutes. Makes 12 rolls.

Muffins and Biscuits

SURPRISING CORNMEAL MUFFINS
2   eggs, slightly beaten
4   tsp. sugar
1   T. salad oil
½   cup self-rising flour
½   cup self-rising cornmeal
¼   tsp. ground caraway seeds
¼   cup instant nonfat dry milk solids
¼   cup warm water
¼   cup shredded cheddar cheese

Combine eggs, sugar, and salad oil; stir in flour, cornmeal, and caraway seeds.

Dissolve dry milk in warm water; add to cornmeal mixture, and stir to mix. Add cheese; stir gently, but do not beat. Spoon into greased 2-inch muffin pans, and bake at 375 degrees for 10 to 12 minutes. Yields 6 muffins.

Baked Varieties

OATMEAL BREAKFAST PANCAKES
In bowl combine 1 cup sifted regular all-purpose flour, 1 cup quick cooking rolled oats, ½ tsp. salt and 2½ tsp. double-acting baking powder. With spoon, slowly beat in 1½ cup milk, then 1 egg and 2 T. melted butter or margarine.

Using a ¼ cup measuring cup as scoop, pour ¼ cup batter onto lightly greased hot griddle. Cook until top is covered with bubbles. Turn, cook until golden. Yields 10-12 pancakes. Keep warm on cookie sheet by covering with foil in oven 200 degrees.

TOASTY-NUT GRANOLA
6   cups uncooked quick or old-fashioned rolled oats
½   cup brown sugar
¾   cup of wheat germ
½   cup flaked or shredded coconut
⅓   cup sesame seed or sunflower seed kernels
1   cup chopped walnuts, pecans, peanuts, or unchopped raisins
½   cup of salad oil
⅓   cup of honey
1½ tsp. of vanilla

Heat oats in shallow baking pan in oven at 350 degrees for about 10 minutes. Combine toasted oats, brown sugar, wheat germ, coconut, seeds and nuts. Add oil, honey, and vanilla; mix to coat dry ingredients. Divide mixture into halves. Return one portion into shallow baking pan and heat at 350 degrees 20-25 minutes, stirring every 5 minutes or so to brown evenly. Cool, then stir until crumbly. Now add raisins, if used. Heat the other half the same way. Makes about 10 cups or 40 servings.

Desserts

Cakes

MOTHER'S POUND CAKE
4   eggs (separated)
2   cups sugar
2   cups flour
1   cup milk
¾   cup Crisco
1   tsp. vanilla
2   tsp. baking powder (rounded)

Cream sugar and Crisco. Add egg yolks separately. Sift flour and baking powder 5 times and add to sugar mixture alternately with milk. Fold in stiffly beaten egg whites. Bake in greased and floured tube pan at 300 degrees for 1 hour.

SHEATH CAKE
In a large bowl mix and set aside:
2   cups sugar and 2 cups flour. In a small saucepan bring to boil 2 sticks margarine, 3 T. cocoa, and 1 cup water.
Pour cocoa mixture over sugar and flour. Mix well and add:
1   egg,
1 tsp. vanilla
½   tsp. cinnamon
½   cup buttermilk

Mix well and bake in well greased 12 x 8 pan for 25-30 minutes at 350 degrees. Immediately upon removing from oven pour on your favorite vanilla sauce.

SOUTHERN BANANA CAKE

1 stick butter
2 cups sugar
½ cup cooking oil
4 eggs
3 cups flour
2 tsp. soda
½ tsp. salt
2 tsp. cinnamon
1½ tsp. cloves
6 ripe bananas (mashed)
1½ cups chopped nuts
1 bottle marachino cherries

Cream butter, sugar and oil. Add eggs. Add sifted dry ingredients. Add bananas. Add cherries and nuts. Bake in tube pan for 1½ hours at 350 degrees. Do *not* open oven door during baking.

DESPERATION CAKE

Beat 1 egg and add ½ cup sugar while beating. Add 1 cup flour mixed with 1 tsp. baking powder and ¼ tsp. salt. Then add ¼ cup milk, 3 T. melted margarine and 1 tsp. vanilla. Bake in greased floured 11" x 7" pan in preheated 350-degree oven 25 minutes. Serve with Vanilla Sauce.

Puddings, Cobblers

POOR MAN'S PUDDING

Mix 4 cups milk with 3 T. regular rice, ½ tsp. salt, ⅓ cup molasses and ½ tsp. cinnamon. Pour into buttered casserole and bake in preheated 300-degree oven, stirring 3 or 4 times during first hour to keep rice from settling, about 3 hours. At last stirring, add 2 T. margarine.

TRIFLE

Place in a deep dish rounds of dry yellow, sponge, or layer cake. Soak with 1 T. rum flavor mixed with one T. water and fruit juice—enough to saturate sponge cake.

Make a jello with water or juice (according to directions on package) and add fruit. When jello and fruit is half set, pour over cake, let it set.

Prepare rich custard with vanilla, banana, coconut, etc., and pour over jello. Let that set.

When custard is set, cover with layer of sliced bananas, cover with whipped cream and garnish.

Cookies

OATMEAL COOKIES
1 cup sugar
1 cup shortening
1 cup raisins (boil in water for 10 minutes)
Pinch of salt
5 T. raisin liquid
1 tsp. soda
2 eggs
2 cups oatmeal
2 cups flour
1 tsp. cinnamon
½ tsp. nutmeg
1 tsp. vanilla
1 cup walnuts or pecans

Cream shortening and sugar; then add raisin liquid and eggs. Sift together the flour, soda, salt and spices and add to mixture. Stir in oatmeal, raisins and nuts. Then add the vanilla. Drop by teaspoons on baking sheets. Bake in moderate oven 350 degrees for 8 to 10 minutes.

FRUIT COCKTAIL COOKIES
Cream:
1 cup shortening
1 cup brown sugar
½ cup white sugar
Add:
3 well-beaten eggs
2 cups fruit cocktail (drained)
½ cup nuts
1 tsp. vanilla
Sift:
1 tsp. soda
1 tsp. baking powder
4 cups flour
1 tsp. cinnamon
1 tsp. cloves

Drop from spoon and bake 8 to 10 minutes at 400 degrees.

Candy

NO COOK OATMEAL CANDY
Mix:
2   cups sugar
1   stick butter
½   cup milk
4   T. cocoa
Cook until it comes to a boil. Boil 1 minute. Remove from heat and stir in:
½   cup peanut butter
1   tsp. vanilla
3   cups oatmeal

Drop from teaspoon onto cookie sheat or waxed paper and allow to cool.

The $1.00 Meal

STUFFED BEEF PATTIES (6 servings)
1½   pounds ground beef
¾   cup grated cheddar cheese
3   T. chili sauce
3   T. drained pickle relish
Salt

Shape ground beef into 12 thin patties about 3½ inches in diameter. Combine cheese, chili sauce and pickle relish. Spoon cheese mixture on 6 of the patties, spreading to within ½ inch of edge. Top these with remaining patties and seal by pressing edges together. Broil 3 inches from heat for about 5 minutes on each side. Season with salt after cooking.

Approximate cost per serving 40¢.

CABBAGE AND CARROT SALAD (6 servings)
2½   cups finely shredded cabbage
1   cup grated raw carrots
1   medium green pepper, chopped
1   tsp. salt
¼   cup mayonnaise

Combine cabbage, carrots and green pepper in a bowl. Sprinkle with salt. Add mayonnaise and blend mixture together by tossing lightly.

Approximate cost per serving 10¢.

OVEN FRENCH FRIED POTATOES (6 servings)
6   medium potatoes cut in strips
1 ½ T. salad oil
Salt

Preheat oven to 450 degrees. Coat potato strips with oil in a bowl. Place potato strips in a single layer in a large baking pan and bake for 35 minutes. Turn once after 25 minutes. Season with salt.
  Approximate cost per serving 10¢.

BLUEBERRY CRUMBLE (6 servings)
1   cup graham cracker crumbs
¼   cup sugar
¼   tsp. nutmeg
3   T. margarine, melted
2   cups frozen blueberries
1   tsp. lemon juice
½   tsp. vanilla extract
½   pint vanilla ice cream

Combine graham cracker crumbs, sugar and nutmeg in a bowl. Add margarine and mix well. Place a layer of blueberries in a greased 1-quart shallow baking dish. Sprinkle with a layer of crumb mixture. Continue layering with berries and crumb mixture until ingredients are used ending with crumb layer. Drizzle with lemon juice and vanilla. Bake in a 350-degree oven for 30 minutes. Serve topped with ice cream.
  Approximate cost per serving 18¢.
TOTAL PER MEAL COST 88¢.

SPINACH SALAD (6 servings)
1   package (10 oz.) fresh spinach
6   raw mushrooms, sliced
2   T. wine vinegar
6   T. salad oil
⅛   tsp. salt
⅛   tsp. pepper
1   T. salad herbs

Wash spinach and shake dry. Tear leaves into bite-sized pieces, discarding stems. Place spinach in a salad bowl. Wash mushrooms and slice them over spinach. Combine vinegar, oil, salt, pepper and herbs in a small jar. Cover and shake until thoroughly mixed. Pour dressing over salad just before serving.
  Approximate cost per serving 26¢.

MINTED LEMON FREEZE (6 servings)

½ cup evaporated milk
1 egg, separated
4 T. lemon juice
½ cup sugar
½ tsp. lemon rind
½ tsp. peppermint extract
Pinch of salt
4 graham crackers, crushed
6 sprigs of fresh mint

Chill milk in a freezer tray until it begins to freeze. Place in mixer bowl and beat at high speed. Add egg white and 2 T. lemon juice. Beat until stiff. Add sugar, egg yolk, remaining lemon juice, lemon rind, salt and pepermint extract. Beat at a low speed until thoroughly blended. Place in freezer tray and sprinkle with graham cracker crumbs. Freeze until firm. Serve garnished with mint leaves.

Approximate cost per serving 13¢.

FRUITED HAM (6 servings)

½ cup regular rice
12 thin slices boiled ham
¾ cup brown sugar
1 tsp. cornstarch
Juice of 1 orange
Juice of 1 lemon
½ cup water
Grated rind of 1 orange
⅛ tsp. ground cloves
½ cup whole cranberry sauce
¾ cup pineapple chunks

Cook rice according to package directions. Place cooked rice in greased 1 ½ quart casserole. Top with ham slices. Combine sugar and cornstarch in saucepan. Add orange and lemon juices, water, orange rind and cloves. Mix well, bring to boiling point, and simmer 3 minutes. Add cranberry sauce and pineapple. Simmer 5 minutes. Pour over ham and bake in 350-degree oven until heated through, about 15 minutes.

Approximate cost per serving 40¢.
TOTAL PER MEAL COST: 79¢.

GRILLED TOMATOES (6 servings)
3   medium tomatoes
Salt and pepper
½ clove garlic, finely chopped
2   T. bread crumbs
1   T. butter or margarine

Cut tomatoes in halves and place on baking pan. Sprinkle with salt, pepper, and bread crumbs. Dot with small bits of butter or margarine. Broil until bread crumbs are brown.

Approximate cost per serving 10¢.

OVEN-FRIED FISH FILLETS (6 servings)
2   fish fillets, fresh or frozen (approximately 1 lb. each)
2   tsp. salt
¾ cup seasoned bread crumbs
¼ cup cheddar cheese grated
¼ cup margarine, melted

Wash fish (frozen fillets do not have to be thawed), salt both sides. Sprinkle a greased flat casserole with half the bread crumbs. Place fish in casserole. Sprinkle cheese and remainder of bread crumbs over fish. Pour melted margarine over dish. Bake in 350-degree oven about 15-20 minutes or until fish flakes when touched with a fork.

Approximate cost per serving 60¢.

AMBROSIA (6 servings)
2   medium oranges, sectioned (or ¾ cup Mandarin oranges)
¾ cup pineapple chunks
2   large bananas, sliced
¾ cup flaked coconut

Combine oranges, pineapple, bananas, and coconut in a serving dish. Chill thoroughly in refrigerator. Serve very cold.

Approximate cost per serving 9¢.

BAKED POTATOES (6 servings)
Wash 6 medium potatoes, prick skin with a fork to let steam escape during baking. Bake in 350-degree oven for about 1½ hours or until potatoes are soft when pressed. Cut criss-cross gash across potato tops and insert 1 T. butter or margarine. Garnish with a sprig of parsley.

Approximate cost per serving 8¢.
TOTAL PER MEAL COST 87¢.

SWISS STEAK (6 servings)

1 ½ pound boneless chuck shoulder steak
¼ cup flour
1 tsp. salt
½ tsp. pepper
2 T. cooking oil
1 can (1 lb. 12 oz.) tomatoes
1 small onion, chopped
½ cup water

Place steak on a wooden board. Slash fat edges to prevent curling. Sift flour, salt, and pepper together. Pound flour mixture thoroughly into steak on both sides with a wooden mallet or the edge of a heavy plate. Heat oil in a heavy skillet, add steak and brown on both sides. Add tomatoes with juice, onion and water. Cover tightly and simmer on top of stove or bake in a 325-degree oven for 2 hours.

Approximate cost per serving 56¢.

THREE-BEAN SALAD (10 servings)

1 can (15 ½ oz.) each green and wax beans
1 can (16 oz.) kidney beans
1 medium onion, chopped
½ cup sugar
⅔ cup vinegar
⅓ cup salad oil
1 tsp. salt
1 tsp. pepper

Drain beans and place in bowl. Add chopped onion. Combine sugar, vinegar, salad oil, salt and pepper. Pour mixture over beans, cover, and refrigerate for at least 12 hours. Serve on lettuce or other salad greens. (This mixture keeps well in the refrigerator for several days.)

Approximate cost per serving 16¢.

BAKED NOODLES (6 servings)

1 package (12 oz.) noodles
1 tsp. salt
2 T. margarine
4 cups boiling water

Place noodles in an ungreased 2-quart casserole. Sprinkle with salt. Add margarine. Pour boiling water over noodles and mix thoroughly. Cover and bake in 325-degree oven until tender, about 35 to 40 minutes.

Approximate cost per serving 10¢.

CRANBERRY BAKED APPLES (6 servings)

6   large baking apples
¾ cup chopped raw cranberries
½ cup sugar
3   T. chopped walnuts
½ cup water

Wash and core apples. Slit the skin around apples about half-way down. Combine chopped cranberries, sugar and chopped nuts. Stuff apples with cranberry mixture. Place apples in baking dish. Pour water around apples to prevent sticking. Bake in 325-degree oven until tender (1 to 1½). Serve warm or chilled.

Approximate cost per serving 17¢.
TOTAL PER MEAL COST 99¢.

EGGPLANT SLICES (6 servings)

1   medium eggplant
2   T. salad oil
2   T. grated cheddar cheese
1   tsp. salt
½ tsp. pepper
1   tsp. thyme

Wash eggplant and dry. Cut it into 6 slices and brush with oil. Place slices on heavy duty foil and broil over gray-hot coals for about 8 minutes. Turn and sprinkle with cheese, salt and pepper. Broil for about 5 minutes longer. Before serving sprinkle with pepper.

Approximate cost per serving 10¢.

GRILLED FISH IN FOIL (6 servings)

2   pounds frozen fish fillets
     (cod, haddock or grey sole)
3   medium onions, sliced thin
3   medium tomatoes, chopped
1   tsp. salt
½ tsp. pepper
Pinch of thyme, tarragon and dried parsley
4   T. margarine

Thaw fish fillets in refrigerator. Place fish on heavy duty foil. Top with onion slices. Add tomatoes, salt, pepper, herbs and margarine. Wrap foil tightly, making sure edges are secure. Grill over low fire (gray-hot coals) for 30 to 35 minutes, turning once half way through cooking.

Approximate cost per serving 60¢.

PASTA SALAD (6 servings)

6 oz. elbow macaroni
2 cups frozen carrots and peas
2 T. dehydrated onion flakes
2 T. dill seed
2 tsp. salt
¼ tsp. pepper
¾ cup mayonnaise
¾ cup milk
6 lettuce leaves

Cook macaroni according to package directions. Drain. Cook carrots and peas in a small amount of water. Drain. Cool macaroni and vegetables in refrigerator. After cooling combine macaroni, vegetables, onion flakes, dill seed, salt and pepper in a large bowl. Add mayonnaise and milk. Mix well. Refrigerate several hours. Serve on lettuce leaves.

Approximate cost per serving 23¢.

STRAWBERRY CREAM PIE (6 servings)

¾ cup reconstituted frozen orange juice, cold
1 envelope unflavored gelatin
¼ tsp. grated orange peel
1 pint strawberry ice cream
1 eight-inch frozen pie shell, baked

Pour cold orange juice into a 1-quart sauce pan. Sprinkle gelatin over juice to soften it. Stir mixture over moderate heat until gelatin dissolves. Remove from heat. Add ice cream and orange peel to hot mixture and stir until melted and smooth. Pour into baked pie shell and chill until firm.

Approximate cost per serving 18¢.

TOTAL PER MEAL COST $1.11.

BRAISED LAMB SHOULDER CHOPS (6 servings)

6 lamb shoulder chops, ½" thick
1½ tsp. salt
½ tsp. pepper
Pinch of garlic salt
1½ T. lemon juice
3 T. water

Brown chops on both sides in a skillet. Combine remaining ingredients and pour over chops. Cover and simmer 30 minutes, turning once after 15 minutes.

Approximate cost per serving 73¢.

MASHED POTATOES WITH CHIVES (6 servings)
6 medium potatoes
½ cup reconstituted instant
    nonfat dry milk (approximately)
3 T. butter or margarine
3 T. dehydrated chives
Salt and pepper

Wash and peel potatoes. Cover with boiling water and cook in covered saucepan until tender. Drain, add butter or margarine, salt and pepper. Mash. Add milk and chives. Whip until fluffy.
    Approximate cost per serving 10¢.

FRENCH GREEN BEANS (6 servings)
2 packages frozen french-style green beans
1 beef bouillon cube
½ tsp. pepper
1 tsp. salt
½ tsp. dried basil

Cook beans according to directions, adding bouillon cube to water. Drain. Season with salt, pepper, and basil.
    Approximate cost per serving 13¢.

QUICK BANANA PUDDING (6 servings)
1 package vanilla pudding mix
3 medium bananas sliced
24 vanilla wafers
½ cup toasted coconut

Prepare pudding according to directions on the package. Place alternate layers of bananas, wafers, and pudding in parfait glasses or serving dishes.
    Approximate cost per serving 16¢.
TOTAL PER MEAL COST $1.12.

TURKEY AND POTATO CASSEROLE (6 servings)

3 T. margarine
3 T. flour
½ tsp. salt
¼ tsp. pepper
¼ tsp. paprika
2 cups reconstituted nonfat dry milk
2 T. chopped green onions
3 cups diced cooked potatoes
3 cups diced cooked turkey
½ cup bread crumbs
2 T. chopped parsley

Melt margarine in a 1-quart saucepan. Blend in flour, salt, pepper and paprika. Gradually add milk and cook, stirring constantly, until mixture thickens and comes to a boil. Remove from heat. Stir in green onions. Pour sauce into a 1½-quart casserole. Add potatoes and turkey. Mix well. Top with bread crumbs. Bake in a 350-degree oven for 30 minutes or until heated through. Serve with chopped parsley garnish.

Approximate cost per serving 69¢.

PEAS AND MUSHROOMS (6 servings)

2 packages (10 oz.) frozen peas
½ tsp. salt
1 small onion diced
1 T. margarine
1 can (4 oz.) mushroom stems and pieces

Cook peas in salted water according to package directions. Drain. Meanwhile, saute onions in margarine until lightly browned. Combine peas and mushrooms with onions.

Approximate cost per serving 18¢.

TOSSED SALAD (6 servings)

1 small head lettuce
½ pound fresh spinach
1 medium carrot, grated
½ cup Italian dressing

Wash salad greens. Drain. Dry on a cloth or paper towel. Tear leaves with fingers into pieces that can be handled easily with a fork and spoon. Place greens in a large bowl, add grated carrots. Refrigerate. Just before serving add Italian dressing and toss lightly.

Approximate cost per serving 17¢.

LOW CALORIE ORANGE WHIP (6 servings)

1 T. plain gelatin
¼ cup sugar
½ cup water
1 can (6 oz.) frozen orange juice
½ cup ice water
⅔ cup instant nonfat dry milk
2 T. sugar
1 T. lemon juice

Mix gelatin, sugar and ½ cup water in a saucepan. Stir over low heat until dissolved. Remove from heat. Stir in undiluted frozen orange juice. Chill until mixture is the consistency of an unbeaten egg white. Put ice water in a small bowl. Stir in dry milk. Beat until peak forms. Beat in lemon juice and remaining sugar. Fold into the gelatin mixture. Chill.
    Approximate cost per serving 11¢.

TOTAL PER MEAL COST $1.15.

PARSLIED CARROTS (6 servings)

8 medium carrots
1 T. margarine
2 T. water
¼ cup chopped parsley

Wash, peel and cut carrots in strips. Place carrots in a greased baking dish, dot with margarine, add water. Cover and bake 1 hour in a 325-degree oven. Garnish with chopped parsley.
    Approximate cost per serving 8¢.

SAVORY PORK CHOPS (6 servings)

6 pork chops
¾ tsp. salt
¼ tsp. pepper
6 thin slices lemon
6 tsp. brown sugar
½ tsp. oregano
½ cup catsup

Place chops in baking dish. Sprinkle with salt and pepper. Top each chop with a slice of lemon and sprinkle with brown sugar and oregano. Pour catsup over chops. Bake for about 1 hour in a 325-degree oven.
    Approximate cost per serving 82¢.

CHERRY COBBLER (6 servings)

1 (21-oz.) can cherry pie filling
½ tsp. vanilla
2 cups biscuit mix
½ cup reconstituted nonfat dry milk
1 T. sugar

Mix pie filling and vanilla in a square pan, 8 x 8 x 2 inches. Combine biscuit mix, milk, and sugar in a bowl. Stir until dough forms a ball and cleans the bowl. Drop dough by spoonfuls over cherries. Bake in a 325-degree oven 35 to 40 minutes or until golden brown. Serve warm.

Approximate cost per serving 20¢.

SPEEDY CHEESEY POTATOES (6 servings)

6 servings instant mashed potatoes
¾ T. dried onion flakes
1 tsp. salt
⅛ tsp. pepper
½ cup grated mild cheddar cheese

Prepare potatoes according to package directions adding onion flakes, salt, and pepper. Spread potatoes in greased baking dish. Sprinkle with cheese. Bake in a 325-degree oven for 10 minutes or until cheese melts.

Approximate cost per serving 10¢.

TOTAL PER MEAL COST $1.20.

Chapter V

Saving Money on Nonfood Items

"Inflation? That's like falling in love. You don't know what causes it and there's nothing you can do about it." [14]

Inflation. Some people think that, like death and taxes, inflation is inevitable. It's not. We created it. We can stop it. We can stop it nationally when you and I stop it personally—in our homes, every day, now.

For openers: (1) Figure out your monthly expenses. Write them down. *Put on paper* what it costs you to live. (2) Keep a flow chart of where your money really goes each month. (3) Plan ahead for purchases. Buy when the sales are on.

Bureau of Labor gives these cost estimates:

COST OF LIVING STATISTICS*

Basics (family of four)	INCOME LEVELS Average Family		
	Lower	Middle	Upper
Food	$3,079	$4,149	$5,280
Clothing/personal care	994	1,413	2,087
Housing	1,957	4,180	6,456
Transportation	541	1,075	2,224
Medical	840	842	878
Income tax	811	2,120	4,590
Social security	596	772	772
TOTAL BASICS	$8,818	$14,551	$22,287

If you don't live in one of America's congested and expensive metropolitan areas, you may find these estimates high. The Bureau of Labor Statistics computes another (and lower) norm, broken down into several categories:

"MODERATE" MONTHLY BUDGETS

SIZE OF FAMILY	PERCENT OF NORM	MONTHLY COST
One parent, under 35, and child	40	$280
One parent, 35-54, and child	57	399
Husband, wife, under 35	50	350
Husband, wife, under 35, one child under 6	62	434
Husband, wife, 35-54, one child, 6-15	82	574
One parent, under 35, two children	67	469
Husband, wife, under 35, two children under 6	72	504
NORM		
Husband, wife, 35-54, two children, 6-15	100	700
Husband, wife, 35-54, three children, 6-15	116	812
Husband, wife, 35-54, four children, 6-15	130	910

(1974)

*New York Times, p. 55, Wednesday, February 5, 1975.

They add this cautionary note:

Large Northern cities especially are more expensive than average. Costs in New York City, Boston, and Hartford are about 10 percent more. Costs in Baltimore, Atlanta, Dallas, Houston, and Orlando, rate 5 to 10 percent below average.

The $700 moderate-cost budget for a family of four does not, of course, include income taxes and social security deductions. If it did, the cost would be $850-$900 a month, over $10,000 a year.

If yours is a four-member family and you are earning well above $10,000, yet find yourself continually in debt, check these common spending leaks (i.e., where your money disappears the quickest and quietest): food, commercial entertainment, transportation, and household upkeep (fuel, utility bills, etc.).

To keep a check on all spending leaks, first prepare a budget *plan sheet* like the one in Appendix "C".

Then, during the course of the month, record all (I mean *all*) expenses. Carry a small memo pad and record all expenses immediately (it's not too small to record and you'll forget if you wait until "later"). Record a cup of coffee, a bus fare, a newspaper, a book of matches—everything. Take care of the pennies and the dollars will take care of themselves.

Pick up a *Ward's Auto Record Book*. It's a sturdy little notepad, costing less than a dollar, to carry around in the car to keep track of all car expenses: gas, oil, repairs, tires, etc. It's especially useful at income tax time.

At the end of the month, take out your memo pad and fill in all your expenditures on the budget *worksheet*. (See Appendix C.) Compare (each month) the worksheet with the plan sheet. It may be drudgery at first but eventually you'll look forward to it, having experienced the relief and power of disciplined spending.

Finances is a family affair. Analyze plan sheet and worksheet with mate and children. Include them in decisions about size and recipients of contributions. The happiest philosophy of money for a family, incidentally, is that *no family is too poor to help others*. Not only does that protect your family from dread feelings of worry and insecurity, but reminds them that money doesn't control them; they, under God's guidance, control the money.

Sidney Margoulis recommends including children in spending and shopping decisions as well as contribution decisions. He recommends that parents take children with them

"I've called the family together to announce that, because of inflation,
I'm going to have to let two of you go." [15]

when they shop and show them how to select values in food,
clothing, toiletries, and other needs. Show them how you keep a
record of your spending and how they can keep their record in a
notebook. One wise mother, says Margoulis, has her children
help with the job of sending out the checks to pay bills each
month, so they know where the money goes and how to take care
of a check book.

Together the members of a family form a co-operative unit,
planning purchases and saving money on dozens of goods and
services.

Shopping with Sense

Know *what* you're shopping for. Otherwise you'll end up like
the drifters in the cartoon.

And know *when and where* to buy it, or you'll be sucked into
sales that aren't sales.

Here are three reminders about sales:

Something labeled "sale" may not be so. To sort the genuine
from the phony, remember: (1) The average supermarket, discount department store, or large drugstore contains over 10,000
items. The store advertises sales on only a *few* things. Their
reason is to lure you in so you'll squander on several of the

10,000 not on sale. (2) Remind yourself *why* you're shopping. It's to buy *necessities*. Most Americans (including you), according to *all market surveys and consumer analyses*, shop for power and relaxation. Owning a new item gives them power, and strolling around colorful, glossy-tiled stores relaxes them. (3) You're *at war* with advertisers—they're out to get you. And they're *professionals*; you're an amateur. They know how to suck cash from your pockets; you and millions of other Americans don't know how to keep it in there.

"Oh, we're not looking for anything in particular, we're just here to spend money." [16]

When to Buy

Buy ahead of time—way ahead.

Dr. Henry Scharles, School of Business Administration, Georgetown University, relates an incident: "There was a sale in the neighborhood store at Eastertime on a lot of kids' clothes. I picked up a number of $10 sweaters for $2.50 each. They are going to be Christmas gifts for some nieces and nephews." Sheer common sense and wise planning.

Mrs. Iris Ellis, author of *Save on Shopping Traveler's Guide*, says that the retail industry makes 30% of its yearly sales in the month before Christmas. "You know you can't get bargains then," she says and suggests that smart shoppers finish the bulk of their Christmas purchases by October at the latest.

Dr. Scharles says that not only lower costs but better service are reasons to shop early: "If you go into an air-conditioner dealer's store in June, they'll hate you. They're up to their necks in customers and they don't need one more. If you come in during the off season, you can get the royal treatment, like the prodigal son returned."

You may never buy an air conditioner, but you get the point.

When to Buy What

Financial Marketing Associates (and others) suggest the following:

Calendar of sales:*

January: After Christmas clearances on toys, decorations, cards, white goods, furs, men's clothing, housewares.

February: Furniture, housewares, mattresses, glass.

March: Pre-season sales on spring clothes. Post-season clearances on winter clothes and sports equipment.

April: Post-Easter sales of clothes. Spring cleaning and a gardening specials. Don't go house-hunting April through September.**

May: A slow month for sales. But you may find some pre-season discounts on summer clothes; also, rugs, carpets, cleaning supplies.

June: Furniture; semi-annual sales of clothing, frozen foods.

July: Mid-year warehouse clearance sales of regular and "as is" merchandise, white goods, unsold summer clothes.

August: End of summer clearances, clearance of current model cars, camping equipment and summer furniture.

September: TV and appliance sales prior to model changes.

October: Summer sports equipment, woman's light coats.

November: Pre-Christmas sales on some items before Thanksgiving.

December: Bad month for sales until after Christmas. May be a good time to shop for a car and house.

---

*From, "How To Be a Better Shopper," Financial Marketing Associates.

**April through September are *not* good months for buying a house. Everyone's looking for a house then, wanting to get settled in for summer or for the school year. Generally, November through February are the months when it's a buyer's market for homes.

Cautions

If you don't need that certain item, it's not a sale. That's rule No. 1 when deciding on a sale or any purchase. Here are several others: Ask yourself these four questions:

1. What is it for?
2. What will it cost?
3. What substitutes are there? (i.e., what else will do the same job?)
4. What will the substitute cost?

Don't buy merchandise out of keeping with your life-style. If you live on an "average" middle-class income, a limousine-type car would be an absurd purchase. Despite the fact that it is on sale, you still can't afford it and you certainly can't afford the upkeep.

If you can afford the sale merchandise and it is something you possibly need, do you have enough room to store it? If not, forget it.

Sales are never for the indecisive. Sales are usually marked "Transactions are Final." Thus you lose all chances of coming back for a refund or exchange. Be sure you need it.

Sales, unfortunately, are sometimes not for the courteous and civil. If it's a good sale, you can be sure the doors will be stampeded at 9:30 sharp by many surging to bargain tables like trail-dusty cattle lusting for water.

Sales are not for you if you're easily persuaded. Chasing after sales makes you vulnerable to "bait" advertising. You'll find yourself lured into a store by values that don't exist, and when you get there, a salesman will persuade you to buy something other than the bargain you came for. Before buying anything, ask yourself: Did I *plan* to purchase this item before I entered the store? If not, maybe you should forget it.

Getting the Best Discount Buys

Maintain a running list of things you need to buy which can be bought in a mammoth discount store (K Mart, Gibson's, Grant's, etc.). There are dozens around larger cities, usually located just off interstates and other main streets. That's a lot cheaper way to buy than running down to the local quick-stop store or supermarket every time you need toilet paper or scotch tape.

Family Circle says there are five other (and less well-known) types of discount houses: buying services, wholesale mail-order houses, catalogue showrooms, co-operatives, and wholesale warehouse outlets.[17]

Buying Services

When you are a "member" (almost all buying services are affiliated with already established organizations), you tell the buying service the make and model of a product you are interested in. The service sends you instructions on how to buy the item from the participating dealer—wholesale or retail—closest to you. Typically, your price will be 25%-40% below official retail price; 6%-10% above wholesale. A typewriter, for example, which retails for $330.00 sells at a discount-house for $259.00, and at a buying service for only $219.95.

Family Circle notes:

> Buying services usually handle only major, brand-name appliances. A number also arrange for the purchase of automobiles, often between $100 and $125 over dealer cost— less than half the usual markup.
>
> For $7.50 a Brooklyn, N.Y., firm, Car-Puter International Corporation, provides exact dealer-cost information on any specified make and model of car, with any combination of available options and accessories. The firm will also act as a buying service, order the car at a guaranteed $125.00 over dealer cost (higher for luxury models or most foreign cars), plus a $10.00 processing fee.

Family Circle says that United Buying Service is the largest and oldest buying service, serving three million members of 1,000 participating organizations. In 1972, it arranged for the sale of $100,000,000 worth of merchandise. There are some drawbacks of a buying service however:

> You may have to specify the make and model of the item you want, and you will have no opportunity to test it out beforehand. Often, you will have to obtain it from a dealer a considerable distance from your home. For repair or warranty work, you may find your local dealer less accommodating than if you had bought it from him. Also, in dealing with wholesalers who must supply regular retail clients with factory-fresh, sealed, in-the-carton merchandise, you may find it more difficult to return or exchange.

Wholesale Mail-Order Houses:

These are high-volume, low-margin versions of traditional mail-order firms. They recruit members at annual rates of between $6.00 and $10.00. They tend to specialize in small, less expensive items, such as jewelry, watches, silverware, china, luggage, toys, small appliance and gift items. Since they are dealers, selling from their own stock of merchandise, their brand-name selection is less extensive than that of a buying service. But in product areas where the two overlap, they are usually quite competitive in price.

The largest mail-order wholesale house is Unity Buying Service Co. in Hicksville, N.Y., with 633,000 members who pay $6.00 in annual dues. It sells goods at 6% over "factory price" as listed in a "confidential booklet" accompanying its catalogue.

Wholesale mail-order houses have the same general problems as buying services, says *Family Circle,* and adds a warning: "Firms charging unusually high membership fees, over $10.00, and promising extravagant savings should be regarded with suspicion."

Catalogue Showrooms:

Once operated by wholesalers in warehouse districts to deal with retail purchasing agents, they are now expanding. The catalogue is lavishly illustrated and features the same sort of items as wholesale mail-order houses. It lists the manufacturer's "suggested retail price" and an easily decipherable "coded" discount price—which you pay. Merchandise can be ordered either by mail (usually for an extra 6% fee) or at a showroom where you write the desired items and catalogue numbers on an order slip and, within a few minutes, pick up the goods. Major credit cards are generally accepted. Repair and delivery service is seldom available. By the end of this year, there are expected to be 1,500 catalogue showrooms in operation, mainly in the East, Midwest, and Southwest, with annual sales of $1.25 billion.

Not everything in the catalogue showroom is necessarily cheaper than a conventional discount. Therefore, look carefully!

Co-operatives:

A co-operative is simply an organization, jointly owned by its members, that uses its bulk, purchasing power to offer members a better deal. The nation's 23,000 credit unions, with some $27 billion in assets, are the largest form of co-ops; some steps have now been taken to liberalize their eligibility rules and expand the financial services they offer. They are farm co-ops, electrical co-ops, housing co-ops. A group of Michigan farmers has for years been buying paint directly from a factory at savings of 60%. A loose confederation of local retail co-ops in the New York area sells goods ranging from tires and hardware to groceries and insurance, often under the co-op house brand, at considerable savings. A co-op member pays a small annual membership fee and receives a refund on his total yearly purchases, based on the co-op's profits.

If you are associated with a university, it may have a co-op bookstore, selling books and other material at below cost. Check with officials of any profession, civic, and trade organizations you belong to, asking what co-op services are available to you.

The section on buying produce described the advantages of a food co-op. You may also wish to see *How to Start Your Own Food Co-op.**

Wholesale Warehouse Outlets:

These are private entrepreneurs who operate out of warehouses and tiny storefronts, dealing usually in major appliances. They rarely advertise and offer few amenities: no showroom or display models, no credit, no delivery except on large items, no repair service. But the savings can be great. I (Chris Welles, the author of the *Family Circle* article) recently bought a 23-inch color TV set from one such outlet in northern New Jersey for . . . just $15.00 (or less than 3%) over the wholesale cost, and at least $60.00 under the best price quoted by the several other area stores.

. . . By far the most publicized wholesale warehouse outlet is Jamaica Gas and Electric, in the borough of Queens, New York City, which deals only with members of labor unions and civil servants. This year J.G.E., which advertises on local TV, will sell $8,000,000 worth of large appliances, mostly TV sets.

Other wholesale-priced, discount-priced outlets include Salvation Army, Goodwill, freight-damaged and rummage-sale stores, as well as the ubiquitous neighborhood garage sales. Quality and price of goods vary greatly but keep looking and you'll find many clothes, appliances, and furniture pieced—up to

---

How to Start Your Own Food Co-op by Gloria Stern, Walker & Co., 720 5th Ave., N.Y., N.Y. 10019.

85% savings and only slightly used.

Discount prices on many goods and services are available to specialized age groups and professional groups. If, for example, you are over 65, a teacher, clergyman, veteran, or writer, you'll find many discounts available just for you. Ask.

If you are new in town, you are eligible to get a book of discount coupons from Welcome Wagon (check with the white pages or call local Chamber of Commerce). A Welcome Wagon hostess will be "right over" to give you a city map, names of area schools and churches, and a book stuffed with coupons for free meals in area restaurants. She'll also have free gifts from area banks, gift shops and department stores, and generous discount certificates for a wide range of purchases.

Contracts and Warranties

Before you sign a contract or warranty, check on the dealer or manufacturer. You do this by calling a government federal hot-line 1-800-638-2666; an operator is available to provide information on nearly all purchases. You can also check on the dealer's or manufacturer's ratings with Dun and Bradstreet.

Be wary of any dealer who doesn't want to extend a contract or warranty or is vague about explaining its features. Find out if the terms of the warranty still apply even if the company should go out of business. Be sure the warranty includes pick-up and delivery charges if the purchase (a large appliance, say) breaks down within warranty time and you have to return it to the dealer for repair. Don't sign any warranty or contract which allows dealer to garnish your wages, should you miss payments or default, or go bankrupt. They, of course, won't use the phrase "garnishing wages" as Sidney Margoulis explains:

> Carefully read the contract you are asked to sign. If it contains a clause to the effect that the buyer agrees not to assert against an assignee (a finance company or bank) a claim or defense arising out of the sale, you had better be sure you are dealing with a reliable seller.

What does the warranty actually cover? Look for these criteria says the Major Appliance Consumer Action Panel (MACAP):

Name and address of warrantor.

Product or specific parts covered and what they are covered for.

Specific time period for which product or parts are covered.

Exactly what the warrantor will do and at whose expense in case of a claim.

Warranty terms given in language that is clear, concise, simple and avoiding legalese.

Exceptions and disclaimers presented prominently as affirmative statements.

Warranty terms stated in printing that is well spaced and easy to read.

Headings or titles presented in a manner that is fully descriptive and accurate.

Additionally, check these out:

Is the service contract or maintenance agreement fairly priced?

Does the service contract merely offer services already given under the warranty?

Would you be expected to start paying finance charges immediately on the service contract, even though it might not become effective until a year after you purchase the appliance?

If it seems like a hassle to check these out before a purchase or signature on a contract, just remember that an ounce of prevention may equal a pound of dollars. Once you've made a purchase or signed a contract and *then* there is evidence of default or deceit, it's costly, time-consuming and frustrating (and sometimes impossible) to get redress. If there is any doubt about the contract or warranty, have a lawyer (yours, not theirs) look at it. It's worth the investment.

Now you tell me! What if I've already been ripped off by a lousy contract? Here are some things you can do for redress. Go right to the top with complaints, says Ralph Nader. If you start at the top, the information will eventually flow down to the right person—and with the force of a presidential directive! If the fault includes false or deceptive advertising, complain both to the federal and state offices of the Attorney General.

If the manufacturer does not honor a warranty or gives unsatisfactory repair service, call or write the Major Appliance Consumer Action Panel, 20 N. Wacker Dr., Chicago, Ill. 60606.

If several others have been fleeced like you, get together as a group, hire a lawyer, and file a class-action suit.

These are *ex post facto* procedures. The horse is already out of the barn. It's better (again) to check thoroughly before purchases are made and contracts are signed.

Buy Products That Are Safe

Each year 20,000,000 Americans are victims of products used in and around the home. 30,000 are *killed* and 110,000 *disabled permanently*. In response to that toll, Congress in 1973 created the Consumer Product Safety Commission (CPSC).

During the past several months, CPSC has done the following:

Banned 13 aerosol spray-adhesive products for six months while a panel of scientists conducted extensive investigation, after initial research had shown a possible risk of genetic damage to future, unborn children of those who use the products.

Warned 1,600 owners of the "Electric Heater Log," a decorative pseudo fireplace, to unplug the units immediately to avoid a possible fire hazard. The manufacturer co-operated with the commission by notifying its distributors and retailers to halt sales of the fireplace.

Cited a TV antenna called "Little Wonder" as a hazard because it contained no built-in safety device to prevent electrical shock and possible electrocution. The commission made sure all antennas were recalled from sale and circulation and that all buyers were reimbursed.

Set mandatory flammability standards for mattresses to insure that they resist ignition from cigarettes and other small heat sources.

Launched a nationwide pre-Christmas campaign to get 1,500 banned toys off the shelves of retail stores and to inform consumers of possible toy-associated hazards.

Developed a new set of mandatory safety regulations for baby cribs. All cribs manufactured after last January 31 must adhere to the new regulations and say so on the crib label.

Beyond these specific actions, the commission has also taken longer-range steps whose impact will be felt in the months and years to come. It has begun the complicated process of developing safety standards for a long and varied list of products used in and around the home. Receiving high priority are architectural glass, football equipment, matches, power lawn mowers and extension cords.

The CPSC also maintains a toll-free hot line (800-638-2666) except in Maryland (800-492-2937). Originally designed to answer questions about toy and crib safety, the toll-free service has been extended to cover all product safety inquiries. It will not discuss particular brands over the phone but will send callers this information by mail.

CPSC, incidentally, also releases a "Consumer Product Hazard Index." Recently, it has listed bicycles, stairs, ramps, landings, and nonglass doors as leading hazards around the home.

Clothes

If you're concerned about keeping up with the latest fashions in clothes (or cars, appliances, furnishings, for that matter), forget about saving money. You don't need this book; you need a bottomless bank account. But if you're sufficiently interested in money-saving to resist ephemeral kicks of fashion, then put into practice the following:

On every clothing purchase, check for durability, fabric, and quality.

Check Salvation Army, Goodwill, rummage sales, garage sales and classified ads ("Clothing for Sale," "Items for Sale" columns), and "reject" or "irregular" racks of stores and factory outlet stores. I've already described advantages of the Salvation Army type stores, but even they can't beat the buys available in garage sales. One will often find, for example, $4 or $3 items of children's clothing (in good condition) selling for 10¢ or 25¢.

Buy sweaters, heavy shirts, and heavy socks comfortable enough to wear around the house. Wearing warm clothes around the house greatly reduces heating costs.

Buy summer clothing in September, fall clothing in December, winter clothing in March, and spring clothing in June or July. Plan ahead.

Socks, particularly children's socks, have a tendency to get lost in the wash. When dirty socks are removed, pin together or place in a mesh bag before they go into the washer. The less socks lost, the less socks bought.

Belts which attach to washable clothing (like bathrobe belts) also have a tendency to get lost (especially kid's belts). Sew washable belts to garments and they won't get lost.

Swap clothes between neighbors and relatives. When *their* nine-year-old boy outgrows his clothes, he'll pass them on to *your* seven-year-old boy, and when your four-year-old girl outgrows her clothes, you pass them on to their two-year-old girl.

Your House: Buying One, Maintaining One

"Beware of small expenses," Benjamin Franklin said, "because a small leak sinks a great ship." Here are several ways to cut expenses around the house.

Kitchen: Don't throw away saucepan lids which have knobs missing. Instead push a sharp pointed screw through the hole and twist a cork onto it. The cork makes a good heat-proof handle.

Don't buy over-gadgeted items like self-cleaning ovens, automatic timers, or ice-makers.

Keep food up and away, out of everyone's sight. The more you see food lying around the more you are tempted to snack and run up bills and beltline.

Use aluminum wrap rather than plastic wrap. Aluminum can be wiped clean and reused.

Never buy kitchen appliances in a supermarket. It's easy to do, but expensive.

Living Room: Check Salvation Army stores for furniture before you invest money at the going retail price. Buy multi-purpose furniture—like sofa beds. Buy furniture that's "Scotch guarded" or made of washable fabrics. Generally, buy furniture that's durable and heavy. It is usually more expensive (tag price), but its durability will pay for itself many times over. One exception: if you have toddlers (or haven't begun a family yet), you might consider cheap furniture during the years the kids are growing up. Unless you plan to keep tiny children chained to their beds, they *will* climb on household furniture sometime, leaving spit stains, urine odors, and nail-and-teeth marks.

Rugs: Check at rug cleaners to see if they have unclaimed rugs. Use carpet remnants (which you can pick up at garage sales or carpet sales) for area rugs and end pieces. Before buying, find out how easy and how expensive it could be to clean or wash rugs.

When you no longer have need for household items (large or small), give them to a local charity and deduct the estimated cost from your income tax.

House Exterior—Painting: Use the same brand of paint each time you repaint (unless earlier brand was clearly unsatisfactory). Scrape and clean surface before painting to insure smooth, durable application. The frequency with which you paint depends, of course, where you live. If you plan to live in a coastal area where salt, wind and sand beat on a house, you may have to paint every two years. Take the cost of painting into account when you buy a house. To prevent a paint job from blistering, paint the north side in the early morning, east side late morning, south side early noon, and west side in the late afternoon. If applying two or more coats, wait two weeks between coats.

Buying a House: How to buy a house is too complex and too broad to cover in this book, but here are a few strategic pointers to start with.

The best time to buy a home is from November-February, generally. Sellers are eager but buyers are few. It's definitely a buyer's market.

Get someone who knows houses to look at a house with you before you buy. Get a builder, carpenter, plumber and/or electrician—someone who has been around houses a lot—to go with you. Offer to pay him for his time and evaluation so he knows you want a deadly serious appraisal and not a superficial, complimentary appraisal of the house you "discovered." If you don't know anyone, check in the Yellow Pages under "Building Inspection Service."

Before you consider a contract for a house or the property on which it's to be located, be sure it contains the following: purchase price; amount of cash down-payment; method and schedule of financing; delivery date of property/house; right to inspect property/house with an expert; right to inspect house while it's being built; delivery of clear title and survey; and firm statement of maximum limit of closing costs. (An unscrupulous builder or realtor can milk you with a long list of at-the-last-minute closing costs.)

Total housing costs (mortgage payments/rent, interior and exterior upkeep, including utilities) should not exceed 20%-25% of total take-home pay. Shop around for best interest rates before buying a home. Check with VA and FHA to see if you qualify for their loans. Check with different banks, savings and loan and mortgage companies to see who offers the best interest rates.

If you're real adventurous, you might want to recycle one as the Archie Barneys did, or collect your own timber and piece it together as others did:

Consider that $15,000 home that Mr. and Mrs. Archie

Barney live in up in Wisconsin, for example. It's actually an abandoned schoolhouse, complete with bell, and there are thousands of such structures in almost every section of every state, now that most of the little country schools have been consolidated.

You can start recycling one of these buildings for yourself or your family by writing to the department of education in the state of your choice. Ask for a list, with addresses, of school administrators. Then pick out the area that interests you most, write to the administrator in charge of the region and ask for information about any schools that may be for sale.

Most of the old educational buildings are sold for sealed bids (that's how the Barneys got theirs) and prices during the last few years have ranged all the way from $100 to $3,500. That's really dirt-cheap, because even the most expensive recycled schoolhouses—those $3,500 ones—are super-bargains when you consider that they have wells, furnaces, and water systems already installed and ready for use. You can move right in, and have a place to live while you're converting the structure into a home.

Let's say you pick up one of those buildings for about $2,000 and spend another $2,000, as the Barneys did, remodeling the structure.

You'll probably find, again, as the Barneys did, that your finished home is easily worth $15,000 or more.

Not bad . . . but another couple up in Washington State did even better. Those folks collected old railroad ties, which they got absolutely free, and constructed their own rustic 2,200-square-foot, three-bedroom home a little at a time during five summer vacations. They just laid the 8 inch by 8 inch ties up like logs and filled in between them with mortar. The finished house is easily worth $20,000 and the shell cost the couple only those five vacations and 300 bucks out-of-pocket money for the mortar.

The Darrell Huff family lives north of San Francisco and they used the same build-it-yourself a little at a time idea to transform two acres worth $5,000 and an average $6,500-a-year income into a house and property worth over $45,000.

The Huff home is a beautiful, rambling, post-and-beam California design with lots of big windows and a huge stone fireplace that Darrell, his wife and children put together with their own hands. Actually, it's the second house the Huffs have constructed this way: The first was built partly with the materials salvaged from a deserted mansion and, when sold, largely financed the fabrication of the second. Darrell made up the remaining dollar slack by writing and selling articles about the family's experiences with do-it-yourself carpentry.

At no time that the Huffs were building that $45,000 equity did their income average over $6,500 a year . . . and, as you probably realize, that's considered by the federal government to be poverty level for four people (there are six in Darrell's family).

If the idea of building or remodeling your own house scares you, you may be relieved to learn that neither the Huffs nor that couple in Washington had any prior construction experience when they started their projects. Darrell had put together a bookcase and dining room table but, as he says, "I found a house easier to build. Tolerances on a home can be fairly large— as much as a quarter of an inch—cabinetwork calls for more precision." [18]

Utilities

Saving on Water Bill

Rockwell International Corporation, largest water meter producer in the United States, says that a pin-hole leak in a water line or a badly leaking faucet can cause your water bill to double. Just a pin-hole leak can mean a loss of *18,000 gallons* of water per quarter, which equals the normal demand from an average home. This means that where water bills are combined with sewage bills, that can amount to the quadrupling of the bill *each quarter*.

Leaky faucets are a culprit too. Drips don't just annoy; they waste water and energy (in the case of a hot-water line). *Money* magazine says: "One faucet leaking hot water at a rate that would fill a coffee cup in six minutes wastes 5,475 gallons in a year; that costs over $9 if you have a gas heater, more than $25 if it's electric."

Saving on Phone Bill

There are at least nineteen ways to cut down on your phone bill:

(1) Avoid paying extra installation charges when you order new phone service. Have all the work done at one time. Changing your mind later will mean extra visits and extra charges. So consider carefully all the different colors and styles, how many phones you want and exactly where you want them installed.

(2) Ask a service representative to explain the different types

of service offered by your local Bell Company. Choose the one which best fits your pattern of calling. If you don't do a lot of calling each month, ask if "budget" or "limited" service is available in your area at a lower rate.

(3) Ask a service representative for a rundown on the specific rates and charges you can expect. Find out exactly what the regular monthly charges will be, and what the one-time-only payments are. Find out whether there are options in your area of paying on a monthly basis, or making a single one-time-only payment, on certain items.

(4) If you are going to be away from home for any extended period of time, a service representative can tell you, based on how long you plan to be away, whether you could save money by temporarily suspending your telephone service.

(5) When moving to a new residence, check with the Telephone Company to see if you are eligible for credit on your bill if you take your present phones along with you.

(6) If you've never had a phone in your name before, or have never established credit, you may be asked to pay a deposit when you order telephone service. But if you establish good credit by paying on time, the company will return your deposit PLUS interest. Call them today requesting return of your deposit.

(7) If a coin phone swallows your money but doesn't give you your call, you're entitled to a refund. Find a phone that works, dial "Operator" and explain what happened. You'll get a refund in the mail. And be a good Samaritan: tell the operator the telephone number and location of the phone that's out of order so they can fix it.

(8) If you reach a wrong number on a long distance call just dialed, don't just hang up. Ask for the area code and the number you reached in error. Then dial "Operator" and report what happened. The operator will have the charge removed.

(9) If you get a poor connection on a long distance call, or get cut off in the middle of your conversation, don't just hang up and call back. The person who placed the call should report what happened to an operator. The operator will issue a credit for the time your call was interrupted.

(10) Call the business office of the Telephone Company for any erroneous charges for long distance calls. A service representative will arrange to get the charge removed.

(11) Save on long distance charges by cutting down on

person-to-person calls. It's true you may not be able to reach the person you want on your first try with a station-to-station call. But in many instances you can make two (or even three) out-of-state, station-to-station calls for what it would cost you to make that one person-to-person call. This is particularly true if you dial your own calls instead of going through an operator.

(12) Dialing your own out-of-state long distance calls is the least expensive way of all. If you don't know the number for a call to a distant city, you can obtain it at no charge to you by dialing the area code (when required) for that city, plus 555-1212, for directory assistance. Then dial direct and save. (All area codes are listed in the information pages at the front of your local telephone directory.)

(13) Make sure you know when dial-direct rates apply before you make your call. They apply on all out-of-state calls to anywhere in the United States (excluding Alaska) if they are completed from a residence or business phone without an operator's assistance. They also apply on calls placed with an operator from a residence or business phone when direct dialing facilities are not yet available.

(14) It's even more important to know the circumstances when direct-dial rates do NOT apply. They do not apply on person-to-person, hotel-guest, credit card or collect calls, or on calls charged to another number, because an operator must assist on such calls. Direct-dial rates do not apply on calls made from coin phones, even those from which you dial the complete number yourself before the operator comes on.

(15) While operator-handled calls cost you more than those you dial yourself, there is one exception. If you run into equipment trouble completing a long distance call you yourself are dialing from a home or business phone, you're still eligible for the dial-direct rate even if you require an operator's assistance. Explain your problem to an operator. If you need help in getting the call through, or in making a satisfactory connection, confirm with the operator that it will be charged at the dial-direct rate.

(16) Save even more on direct-dial by making your out-of-state long distance calls within the time periods when rates are lowest. The lower rates for out-of-state calls made in the evening, on the weekends or late at night are described in the call guide in the front of your local directory.

(17) Long distance calls made *within your state* often have

their own special low rates. Check carefully in the call guide in the front of your local directory for a description of when to save on calls within your state.

(18) If you're concerned about avoiding added charges on any long distance call, don't guess how long you've been talking. Time yourself, so you can finish your call before overtime rates apply. To save even more time and money, *jot down what you want to say before you dial.*

(19) Before you go ahead and place a long distance call to a business, check first to see if they have a toll-free number. You can recognize it because it has an 800 prefix instead of a regular area code. If they have one, it's usually displayed in their advertising, or you may find it listed in your own local telephone directory. If so, the call's on them, and you save.

Cooking, Heating, and Lighting: Saving on Energy at Home

Food Preparation

Oven Use

Bake more than one thing at a time in the oven and do not unnecessarily open and close the oven door.

Cook an entire meal, including vegetables, in the oven simultaneously. Place vegetables in oven-proof containers.

Warm plates and precooked foods, like rolls, with the remaining oven heat after main meal is removed.

Use electric bun warmer to keep a meal warm.

Use toaster oven instead of large oven whenever possible.

Wrap hot foods in aluminum foil to keep warm instead of using the oven. Foil will hold heat up to one-half hour.

Instead of cooking every day, cook only three days a week and store extra meals carefully and properly. Merely heat and serve the extra meals on noncooking days.

Use left-over heat from prior oven cooking to toast stale bread and make bread crumbs.

Self-cleaning ovens should be wiped clean immediately after use and the self-cleaning unit used while the oven is still hot.

Note: Do not install refrigerators or freezers near range, radiator, heaters, or sunlit areas.

Range Top

Use "double boiler" top/bottom for separate items to be cooked at the same time.

Use pressure cooker whenever possible.

Cook vegetables in covered pans and use as little water as possible for quickest results.

Heat only as much water as you need.

Cut vegetables and potatoes into small pieces for fast cooking.

Heat enough water in the morning to make both coffee and the day's gelatin desserts.

Cooking Tips

When boiling water, start with hot water from the faucet. Also, turn off unit when first steam vapors appear; residual heat from the element will complete the boiling.

Use high heat only to bring food to a boil then switch to lowest setting needed.

When roasting or baking, use oven vent for prethawing frozen foods, warming dishes, drying washed metal objects, etc.

Range top heating-rings in use should not exceed the width of the pan.

Use outdoor grills when possible.

Thaw or partially thaw frozen foods before cooking (check directions).

Cook enough vegetables, such as potatoes, at one time for several meals. Refrigerate extras until needed.

Disconnect or turn off a cooking appliance or oven a short time before food is done. Residual heat will complete the cooking. (Careful if it's a delicate cake!)

Use covered frying pan to cook "one dish" meals on a large surface unit.

Making Coffee

Instant coffee: Pour heated water into a thermos for second and subsequent cups.

Store perked coffee in thermos bottles for later use—tastes better, too! Doesn't get bitter.

Use a small plug-in heater for a cup of hot water instead of a range unit.

Small Appliances

Use nonelectric mixers, knives, can openers, etc., when possible.

Use small appliances in place of major ones whenever possible.

Use a slow-cooking, low-heat "crock" pot for casseroles.

Food Preservation

If your refrigerator has a butter softener, set it on "soft." Soft butter or margarine spreads thinner.

Keep the rubber seal (gasket) on the refrigerator/freezer door soft by washing occasionally with a good detergent.

Cool beverages in winter by placing in a cold but not freezing porch or storage area.

Prepare after-school snacks for teenagers before they get home. Prevents the constant opening and closing of the refrigerator door.

After shopping, separate perishables and nonperishables. Put refrigerator items away all at once.

Cover refrigerated liquids to prevent moisture from escaping. Excess moisture causes frost-free refrigerators to work harder.

Keep a current list of foods in freezer taped to freezer. Prevents opening freezer door to search for things you may not have.

Check manual to be sure your freezer is operating at the proper temperature.

Laundry and Dishwashing

Washing and Drying

Wash and dry clothes only when you have a full load.

Use cold water and cold water detergents for clothes washing whenever possible.

Soak clothes overnight before washing.

Cut back on clothes washing time for small loads or slightly soiled ones.

Clean lint filter each time before operating dryer.

If drying more than one load, remove one before the dryer stops (eliminating one cool-down cycle).

Occasionally check dryer air vent to make sure it's not clogged.

Hang clothes to dry; use dryer only on wet or freezing days.

Ironing

When nearly through ironing, disconnect iron and use for remaining small items. Save ironing until you've several things to iron.

Reflect heat by placing a piece of aluminum foil under the top cover of your ironing board.

Iron clothes as soon as they come out of the dryer or off the line. Fewer wrinkles mean less ironing.

Use warm water instead of cold in your steam iron.

Use more no-iron synthetic fabric clothes.

Mending

Mend by hand.

Cleaning

Use carpet sweeper or dry-mop daily. Vacuum only once a week.

Empty vacuum cleaner bags before they are overloaded.

Dishwashing

Dishwasher should have full load before using.

Open door to air-dry dishes when washing cycle is over.

If necessary to rinse off utensils or dishes before placing in dishwasher, use cold water instead of hot. (They'll get the hot treatment in the dishwasher.)

Better yet, hand wash dishes instead of using dishwasher. When hand-washing dishes, rinse all at one time with hot water.

Comfort and Personal

Keep bedroom cool and pile on blankets.

Close doors and lower thermostats in unused rooms in electrically heated home.

Set home-heating thermostat at 68 degrees and wear a sweater if cool. At night, lower to 55 degrees.

In summer evenings, use a window fan blowing out instead of air conditioning to cool house.

Keep small timer in bathroom to time showers.

Use "plastic wrap" around windows as weather stripping.

Close chimney damper when fireplace is not in use to prevent drafts and heat loss.

Seal all drafty areas in foundation.

Proper control of humidity allows more comfortable and more efficient heating. Airborne moisture particles distribute heat more evenly throughout a house.

When entertaining during the heating season, lower thermostat before guests arrive. People generate heat.

Arrange furniture in winter so as not to block heating units or vents. Shorten curtains so as not to restrict air flow from vents.

In cold weather leave oven door open after baking to allow heat to circulate.

Use only one exterior door in winter.

Place air conditioner on shaded side of house. Expel warm air from upper parts of house.

Weatherstrip all doors and windows. (Tight fitting storm windows can reduce heating fuel consumption by 15% to 25%.)

Bathroom exhaust fans connected to light switches should be disconnected and equipped with separate switches.

A fine spray nozzle in the shower uses less water.

Showers use less hot water than baths.

Clean or change furnace air filters regularly.

Use storm windows in summer along with air conditioners.

Window mounted or thru-the-wall air conditioners need weather stripping or caulking to operate efficiently.

Adjust air conditioner to highest room temperature that is comfortable. (78 degrees is probably cool enough.)

Keep all windows and doors closed when operating air conditioner.

Home Entertainment

TV

Disconnect "instant-on" TV's when not in use or install a switch in the power cord.

Use a black and white TV.

Don't leave TV or radio on when no one is watching or listening.

Limit TV viewing hours for family.

If you're apt to fall asleep watching late shows on TV, install or use automatic TV shutoff.

If you have two TV sets and two groups are watching the same program, turn one set off.

When TV is on, lower room light level.

Rediscover parlor games to limit the amount of TV watching.

Encourage children to do other activities (outdoors as well as in) to restrict TV use.

Read more—watch TV less.

Lighting

Turn off lights when leaving the room or when room is not in use.

In winter, keep shades up and drapes open during sunny days, but closed at night to save heat.

In summer, shades drawn over sunny windows will help cool the house.

Use small-wattage bulbs or "nite-lites" for casual lighting.

Eat dinner by candlelight.

Use only one bulb in an appliance or bathroom medicine cabinet.

Be sure closed doors with automatic light switches are closed.

Use low-wattage table lamps instead of ceiling lights.

Turn off outside post lights after company arrives and turn them on as they leave.

Use fluorescent lights instead of incandescent when appropriate.

Use 3-way lights at lowest setting whenever possible.

Keep a "lights-left-on money jar." When a family member leaves the lights on, he or she has to put 5¢ in the jar.

Teach children to use lights only when they need them and to turn them off when not needed.

Clean, and keep clean, all lamp shades, reflectors, and light bulbs for better illumination.

Place printed card over an electric light switch: "Turn me off when not needed."

Everyone read in the same room if ceiling light is used.

If one cellar light switch turns on all lights, replace with individual chain-pull switches for each bulb.

Turn off aquarium light at night.

Some Rewiring

Have dimmers installed, especially in dining room ceiling light.

Use switches with red pilot or indicator lamps to signal that a closet or cellar light is on.

If you must leave post lights on all night, put in a photocell so that they will go off at dawn.

Have fluorescent lamps installed where possible.

Decorating and Modernizing

Now

Keep drapes closed at night.

Use sheet plastic on interior window frames to act as an extra storm window.

Future

Be conscious and aware of waste. Check consumer reports and buy quality and efficient appliances.

Buy drapes with foam backing to block drafts.

Use light or transparent lampshades.

Use light and bright colors for room decoration (improves lighting).

Use mirrors for light reflection.

Use storm windows.

Insulate entire house, or at least ceiling areas exposed to roof.

Locate heating and cooling devices so they don't work against each other (e.g., keep refrigerator away from range).

Insulate hot-water pipes.

Install a removable plywood closure (painted black) on the front of your fireplace when you're not using it to block the chimney draft.

Install window awnings to reduce heat buildup.

Install additional louvres in ranch home attics for increased ventilation and more efficient air conditioning operation.

Use discarded bicycle innertubes to weatherstrip the bottom of garage doors that are not flush with the garage floor.

When garage is under house, insulate ceiling.

Install wall-to-wall carpeting to help insulate floors.

Entertainment, Recreation

If you spend a lot of money for tickets or toys for family

recreation, you're just not trying very hard. And if a lot of your entertainment is sitting stone-faced in front of a TV, you're not thinking very hard.

Ask your local Chamber of Commerce and state travel/tourist bureau for a list of places and things to do in your area. Many are free and all provide warm family-time together. Look for museums, zoos, exhibits, concerts, plays, lectures, literary films, and tours. If you live near a college, ask for their calendar of activities. Check local paper under the "What's Going On" (or similar) column.

Take a walk, ride bikes, read, bake bread, build a snowman, build sandcastles, plant a garden, pick apples, visit a rest home (older people love to see young children) and feed the pigeons together. Don't cop out by "buying" the most convenient sort of entertainment.

A few movies are worth seeing. When you go, go during afternoon hours when lower matinee fares are in effect. Ask the theater if they give a discount for your professional or age group. (Discounts are sometimes available for veterans, students, senior citizens, clergymen and others.)

Don't buy "snack-stuff" in the theater. A box of popcorn in the theater costs 50¢! For 50¢, you can buy a bag of popcorn kernels and make four gallons of popcorn!

When traveling with the kids, fix food ahead of time so you won't have to throw away dollars for fat-laced hamburgers and cardboard french fries. For snacks, prepare apple wedges, carrot fingers, celery sticks and crackers. They are cheaper and— equally important—kinder on the teeth than cakes, cookies, candy and gum.

Travel and lodging expenses can be greatly reduced by joining Youth Hostels Association (and you don't have to be a "youth" to join). A cheap vacation can be arranged by switching homes with someone else in a different part of the country, arranged by Pan American Home Exchange Club of New York, 663 5th Avenue, New York, N.Y. 10022. The address for Youth Hostels Association is 20 W. 17th Street, New York, N.Y. 10011.

Toys

Make your own "Play-Doh" or "Fun-Doh." Here's a recipe:

2   cups flour
1   cup salt
Coloring
Water
¼   cup oil

Combine flour, salt and oil. Add water a tablespoon full at a time and knead. Add coloring. Store in refrigerator.

Use old toothbrushes for doll's hair brush.

Get big cardboard boxes from furniture stores, appliance stores, and supermarket. Give a kid a cardboard box that a refrigerator or stove was crated in and he'll explore it for days. Smaller children have ample room to explore in a box that paper towels and toilet tissue were packed in.

Save paper towel and toilet tissue cylinders and spools. They make excellent telescopes, trumpets and toy wheels.

Make your own masks and costumes from paper sacks. "Make & Do" volume of *Childcraft* (available in all libraries) shows you how.

Save old magazines and newspapers for kids to cut up for collage projects and scrapbooks.

A tire store will practically give you old tires. Huge ones (from tractors, etc.) can be laid flat on the ground and filled with sand for excellent sandboxes. Smaller ones can be used for swings or rolling by hand.

Save your milk or juice waxed-cartons and quart plastic jugs. Line them up for bowling pins, a good outdoor or indoor game.

Divide children's toys into two lots, Lot A and Lot B. Put Lot B away, out of children's sight. In two months take out Lot B and they will be delighted with the "new" toys they rediscovered. Then put Lot A away for two months. Alternate lots every two months and kids will keep on rejoicing with their "new" toys, instead of being bored by seeing the same toys all the time.

If kids (or you, for that matter) like certain wholesome magazines, let relatives know. They are always searching to find an appropriate gift for birthdays and Christmas. You'll save the expense of the subscription yourself, give the child the magazine he enjoys, and—most important—give a relative the satisfaction of knowing he bought a gift that was appreciated.

When you do buy toys, check the Salvation Army, Good-Will, etc., stores first.

Toiletries and Paper Products

Soap

Hand soap. Use two bars. Allow a wet bar (out of which chunks are easily removed) to dry and harden before using again. Buy cheap, non-famous brands which come six or twelve to a package. Don't throw soap chips away. Put in plastic squeeze bottle and leave near sink for kids' hand washing. Or put in open-mouth bottle for kids to use as their soap supply for blowing soap bubbles. Use soap instead of shaving cream; lather well and you will get a smooth, clean and quick shave.

Laundry and dishes. Use concentrated, heavy-duty, bio-degradable detergents. The box price is more expensive, but since you use a lot less (Amway, for example, calls for only one capful per load), you save money in the long run. Heavy-duty detergents are truly concentrated, so it's better to use a little less than a little more.

If you use electric dishwashing soap, beware! It's lethal. Just a few grains on your eyes or tongue can burn enough to scar. Many children have had throats or stomach walls eaten and burned by ingesting electric dishwashing detergents. Keep them high!

Toothpaste. Use a coffee can key to place at end of tube to keep rolling it up as it empties.

Paper

Don't buy paper products in a supermarket.

Buy paper towels sparingly, if at all. Many jobs done with paper towels can be done with rags, which are washable and reusable.

Don't buy paper lunch sacks. Use plastic bread bags or small paper sacks which you've saved from grocery purchases. Or buy a small lunch kit (with thermos) which pays for itself many times over.

When buying paper products, check with wholesale house first. If they'll sell you a case direct, it is much cheaper for you in the long run. If they will only sell in lots of several cases, get together with neighbors, pool your money and share your purchases.

Don't buy paper which you know you'll use almost exclusively for scratch paper. Ask librarians, printers, teachers, secretaries, etc., to save scratch paper for you.

Professional Services Expenses
(Medical, Legal, Insurance)

Medical Expenses

If you are living on welfare, your medical needs are taken care of at the medical facilities welfare designates. Otherwise, *get health insurance—today.*

An extended illness or injury will run up $10,000 in bills easily, severely crippling family finances. When you are sick or injured, you don't need the additional problem of money worries. An investment of $15-$50 a month for health insurance alleviates money worries.

Here are several tips on saving on medical expenses, including health insurance:

Reduce big doctor bills by phoning instead of going to his office. Often a doctor can give you advice on the phone and save you and him time. However, don't put off seeing a doctor just to save a few bucks. Sure, some people have lived to 100 without ever seeing a doctor, or so they claimed. But you don't hear much about the many more people who do not live so long and wish—often too late—they *had* seen a doctor in time.

Have your own family doctor. It's particularly important today as our national supply of family doctors has shrunk to an all-time proportionate low (fewer than 70,000) while our population soars. The result: In an emergency more and more people find that doctors are unavailable. "Try the hospital emergency room," they're told.

A family doctor not only gives you personal service, but often can save you time and money by knowing your medical history and being armed with your family's medical record. This can mean a speedier diagnosis as well as sometimes avoiding expensive tests. A family doctor may be unnecessary, however, if you belong to a good group-medical-prepayment plan.

Get a regular medical checkup. This is stock advice, true, but preventive measures are more important than ever in these days of fewer doctors, crowded hospitals and soaring medical costs. An annual checkup is especially recommended for small children and everyone over 35. The cost is small—usually $35 to $85—

and the benefits are large, since early detection of incipient trouble, especially with your heart, lungs, eyes and other such vital organs, often can mean quick and relatively inexpensive control. It could even save your life, as in the early detection of cancer of the breast or prostate, two of the most common cancers which show remarkable recovery rates if found early. Cancer is our country's second biggest killer, with heart disease first.

Discuss the fee before the bill comes. Most doctors welcome this. Determine what special treatment or an operation will cost. If you're financially strapped, tell the doctor so. In many such cases, he'll reconsider his fee. Also ask what you can do to keep down the cost. To check on typical fees for a specific operation or treatment, call your local medical society. That's also where to call if your bill seems high or if you have a complaint (though not all medical societies will respond satisfactorily). Overall, the best medicine for inflammation of the bill (one of the most widespread medical problems) is to discuss the charge beforehand.

Keep down hospital costs. If you must go in, get out fast. The sooner you're out, the greater the relief when the bill comes, especially since the total bill can hit the $100-a-day level. That doesn't include doctors' fees, by the way.

Discuss the choice of a hospital with your doctor. A large medical center or university hospital may offer the most modern facilities and services, but it's usually necessary only for special treatment or a really serious condition. You often pay considerably less in a perfectly good community hospital that offers excellent, if not top-notch, facilities for most routine operations and hospital care. Also ask your doctor about the available choice in community hospitals, considering the best for your purpose, as well as price and convenience.

Don't check into a hospital early on a weekend, when few staff people are there. Most serious tests and other work are not done till Monday morning, but you still pay the full rate every day. Check in between Sunday evening and Friday morning, if possible. Schedule a hospital stay for summer or before Christmas, when most hospitals are uncrowded and the best, most economical rooms are most likely to be available. You're also likely to get the best attention at such times.

Then tell your doctor you want to get out fast. You can always return for a special check or test on an outpatient basis. If you require extended hospital convalescence, inquire about being moved to a "halfway house," such as an accredited nursing home or a motel-like, intermediate-care convalescent hospital section. You get all the necessary professional care at 50 to 75 percent of the daily hospital rate, sometimes less. More and more hospitals provide such highly sensible facilities.

Be a "vertical" rather than a "horizontal" patient. More and more medical tests and treatment that formerly required hospitalization are now done on an out-patient basis in a hospital, clinic or doctor's office. Even tonsils are being removed that way, thus sharply reducing the time and cost of a hospital stay. Talk this over with your doctor. Formerly, this was unwise financially because insurance generally covered only treatment in a hospital, but more and more insurance plans now cover the same treatment done in a clinic, doctor's office or at home. Check your policy for this.

If you already have health insurance, be sure it is up-to-date. Four out of five Americans have health insurance, but much of it pays according to pre-inflation medical costs. Many policies, for example, will pay you a mere $10 to $20 a day for your hospital room, though such charges usually are much more. That's just one example of ineffective health insurance.

The best kind of policy stipulates that the insurance company will pay the standard semi-private room rate and not a fixed amount, and it will also pay standard doctor and surgeon charges. Check your policy for such provisions; if necessary, switch to up-to-date insurance. Other important points to look for: Insurance for a young family should provide mothers with obstetrical care and cover babies from "moment of birth" (not after a certain age in days); cover children until age 22, not 19 (which leaves college-age children unprotected); cover tests and services provided in a doctor's office (rather than cover you for hospital care only); and older people should have special coverage for potential prolonged treatment. To protect against a catastrophic medical bill, consider the purchase of a "major medical" insurance, which can cover you for up to $10,000, $20,000, or more in medical expenses.

Get group insurance whenever possible, by far the best buy in health insurance. You get it from an employer, labor union, professional society or other such group. Best known and among the best buys is a group Blue Cross policy covering hospitalization, and group Blue Shield covering doctor and surgeon bills; or a combination of the two. Usually better, though less widely available, is a prepaid group practice plan; it generally costs a family from $15 to perhaps $30 a month, but it covers most medical bills and surgeon's fees you are likely to have, though not always hospital charges.

If you are self-employed, you may want to join up with thousands of other self-employed people who pool their money to form group insurance services. One such service is Small Business Service Bureau, Inc., 544 Main Street, Box 1441, Worcester, Massachusetts 01608. (National toll free number: 800-255-7312. In Massachusetts: 756-3513)

Save on drugs. Don't be "drug happy" and don't insist that the doctor give you fancy medicine you don't need. To save on this third biggest category of medical costs, shop among drugstores for the lowest prices, particularly for nonprescription drugs. Take advantage of low-cost drug rates offered by certain health plans, unions and such groups as the American Association of Retired Persons. Ask your doctor to specify a good "generic" drug on your prescriptions rather than a higher-priced brand name. Remember, however, that a special brand-name drug sometimes may be better or have greater strength, for example, and therefore be worth its extra cost.

Use your community health facilities. They often offer free chest X rays, vaccinations and other free or low-cost services, and this is not charity. Such services are especially available for persons with handicaps, mental illness, alcoholism and drug addiction. They can do much good, and stop your medical bills from skyrocketing. (You can, for example, get your child's preschool innoculation at a community health center. Your taxes already paid for them.) Get more details from your public health department.

Insure your blood supply. In a real emergency, such as an open-valve heart operation, you might need as much as 30 to 40 pints of blood, at $25 to $35 a pint. Give a pint of blood a year to blood banks, however, and you and your family later get all the blood you need at no charge. Call the Red Cross or your local hospital.

Take *all* allowable tax deductions for medical expenses. Not everyone does. Eligible deductions which people often miss on their income-tax returns include: travel cost to and from the doctor's office, hospital or any other place for medical reasons; medical bills paid for dependents, such as a child away at school; money spent for orthopedic shoes or other physical support or garment; hearing aids; and dental costs.

Always check your medical bills. Everybody (or nearly everybody) is human and makes mistakes; even nonhuman computers make them. Be sure that you don't pay for an item covered by your insurance. Don't go overboard for unnecessary private nurses; use part-time visiting nurses for at-home nursing care. And don't panic if you're hit with an astronomical medical bill. Talk it over with the doctor or hospital people. Nearly all of them will work out a payment schedule that you can meet over a period of time.

Get a good medical book or two, which can help considerably, such as the new book, *How To Reduce Your Medical Bills,* by Ruth Winter, $5.95; the old, reliable Dr. Spock's *Child and Baby Care** and *The Complete Medical Guide* by Dr. Benjamin F. Miller. Know how to *find* and *keep* a good physician. That saves money and worry, according to a *New York Times* series on physicians in the United States.

The *Times* advises:

> Select a doctor while you are healthy, when you can think clearly and have the time to evaluate his competence, rather than when you are sick or faced with a medical emergency. The first visit to a new doctor should be for a routine check-up.
>
> Choose a family doctor to be your regular physician—an internist or specialist in family practice (and a pediatrician or family practitioner for children). Do not choose as your family doctor a surgeon, gynecologist or other specialist who focuses on only one aspect of medical care.
>
> It is usually unwise to refer yourself to a specialist without first seeking the advice of your family doctor. The eye problem you take to an ophthalmologist could be a result of diabetes.
>
> Do not choose a doctor solely on the basis of recommendations of friends or neighbors. Although their impressions of the doctor may be valuable, they are probably no more able than you are to evaluate his competence. Moreover, a doctor who can adequately treat the ordinary illnesses your friends may have may be ill-prepared to handle more specialized problems.

---

*To allay your fears: Dr. Spock does *not* advocate permissiveness. He does advocate making the punishment fit the crime, meaning that sometimes spanking is appropriate and sometimes it isn't, he says.

One good way to find a doctor is to call a nearby medical school or medical school-affiliated hospital. Ask for the appropriate department—family medicine, internal medicine, pediatrics—and obtain the names of department members who see private patients. Such doctors are more likely to keep their medical knowledge current.

Before making an appointment, check the professional credentials of the doctor you are considering. Determine where and when he did his residency (postgraduate) training, if he is certified by one of the 21 American specialty boards and if he holds teaching, research or other positions. These facts can be obtained by consulting the "Directory of Medical Specialists" or the "American Medical Directory," which are found in most libraries, or by asking the doctor or his assistant.

Check on the doctor's hospital affiliations, which are listed in the aforementioned directories and, for New York doctors, in the "State Physicians Directory." If possible, choose a doctor who holds an appointment at a hospital affiliated with a medical school because of the superior training the staffs at these institutions generally receive.

In general, avoid doctors without any hospital affiliation or doctors who only have appointments at small, private, profit-making hospitals. Dr. Arthur Levin, a New York City pediatrician, says that hospitals with fewer than 100 beds—and there are more than 3,000 of them in the country—have death rates 40% higher than other hospitals when the severity of their cases is taken into account.

Consider choosing a doctor in a medical group or large partnership. Such doctors are more likely to have screened one another for quality and are inclined to consult with one another in difficult cases.

Ask important, practical questions beforehand. What are the doctor's fees (if they are not to your liking, this could become a source of discontent), his office hours and location and, if you are an invalid, does he make house calls? Except for patients who cannot leave their homes, house calls are considered by most physicians to be an inefficient and inadequate way to practice quality medicine.

If you have no regular doctor and you are suddenly faced with an illness that requires immediate care, Dr. Levin says it is better to go to the outpatient department of a teaching hospital than to rely on picking a name out of the Yellow Pages soliciting the advice of a friend.

Dr. Levin also cites some "red herrings"—bad reasons for choosing a doctor that have nothing to do with his ability. The best doctor, he insists, is not necessarily one who is well known or who treats famous patients, who has a large practice or who makes you wait weeks for an appointment or requires you to sit hours in his office on the day of your appointment.

A further aid to finding a physician may be a directory of physicians compiled by a local public-interest group. The directories list cooperating physicians' training, credentials, fees, office hours, Medicare and Medicaid participation and other important facts about their practices. About 30 such directories have been prepared for communities around the country, including, in New York, Brookhaven, L. I., Queens and Binghamton, and Albany and Tompkins counties. There are none yet for New Jersey or Connecticut. The Health Research Group, 2000 P Street N.W., Washington, D.C. 20036, can tell you if there is a directory for your area.

Evaluating Health Care:

Once you have chosen a doctor, the next step is to evaluate the care he gives you.

Among the factors that health-care experts suggest you consider are the following:

Does the doctor act as if he knows what he is doing, or does he seem vague, careless or inefficient? Is his office orderly? Does he keep careful records about you and consult them at each visit, or does he ask you to recall what happened at previous visits?

Did your doctor do a thorough "workup" at your first office visit? The workup should include a complete personal and family medical history with precise questions (not "How are your bowels?" but "Have you had any recent diarrhea, constipation, blood in your stool?"), a careful physical examination with your clothes off, checking all parts of your body (including the inside of your mouth), and routine laboratory tests of blood and urine, plus any special tests your history may suggest.

The physical also should include a digital rectal examination for men and a Pap smear and manual pelvic examination for women unless they are regularly examined by a gynecologist.

Your history may be taken by a trained assistant, then reviewed by the doctor, who may ask you further questions. In giving a history, it is in your interest to reveal all pertinent facts, including any emotional problems or personal difficulties, that could affect your health or your doctor's treatment of you.

Do you like the doctor and does he seem to like you? Dr. Marvin S. Belsky, a New York internist, insists that compassion is as important as competence in good medical practice. Your doctor should be someone in whom you feel comfortable about confiding, especially since more than half of the problems you bring him are likely to have an emotional component.

Does the doctor treat you as a rightful participant in your health care, or does he assume a patronizing "I'm the expert, you're the patient" attitude and seem resentful of any knowledge you may have about medicine?

Does the doctor spend enough time with you, or do you feel that he rushes you? Does he reach for his prescription pad before you've finished describing your symptoms or before he examines you?

Does your doctor give you a complete diagnosis? Dr. Levin contends that the use of a symptom, such as anemia or high blood pressure, as the label for your illness is inadequate. What is the cause of the symptom? Is the anemia due to a dietary deficiency, internal bleeding, an inherited blood disease or what? The treatment will differ depending on the cause, and simply treating the symptom without determining the cause could threaten your life.

Does the doctor emphasize preventive medicine, advising you about your diet and weight, exercise patterns and other living habits, such as smoking? And does the doctor set a good example in these areas? An emphasis on preventive health care includes a periodic reminder to return for a routine check-up and the use of detection tests, such as a manual breast examination for women and a proctoscopic (rectal-colon) examination for all patients aged 45 or older.

When the doctor recommends treatment with drugs or surgery or a nonroutine diagnostic test (particularly one that requires hospitalization), does he explain his reasons and the risks and benefits of the recommended procedure as well as the alternatives to it?

Under certain circumstances, it is advisable to get a second opinion from another doctor. According to Dr. Levin, these situations include failure of the doctor to make a definite diagnosis within a reasonable time period (say, two or three visits when you are told you have an illness with a serious prognosis; when you are told you have a rare condition, in instances when your disease is emotionally caused, and when surgery is recommended for treatment or diagnosis.) Under such circumstances, a doctor should not feel threatened when you tell him you want another opinion.

Should you decide to switch to another doctor, you have the right to have all your records sent to your new physician.*

---

*"How Educated Patients Get Proper Health Care," *New York Times*, January 30, 1976, pp. 1, 10.

You may find either of the following books also useful in the selection process: *Talk Back to Your Doctor* by Dr. Arthur Levin and *How to Choose and Use Your Doctor* by Dr. Marvin S. Belsky and Leonard Gross.

Legal Expenses

Someday you will need a lawyer.

Check with your professional, trade, or civic organization to find out if they offer an (increasingly popular) prepaid legal plan.

Don't hire a lawyer simply because he is a neighbor, first in the Yellow Pages, gets his name in the paper a lot, or fills a classy office. Call the local bar association. They will give you a name from their referral list and (maybe) his specialization and professional rating. For a token $10.00 fee, he'll talk to you for thirty minutes to an hour to determine if you really need a lawyer.

Note: the qualification for a lawyer's being on the referral list is simply that he asked to be on it. Beyond referral from the bar association you should ask neighbors and friends about lawyers they've used. Find out as much as you can about him before consulting.

When consulting, clarify his pleading of your case and fees (most lawyers work on a fee of 33% of the settlement or a straight $25-$50 per hour). Whatever fee you agree upon, write it in separate contracts which both sign in the presence of witnesses. Keep a copy for your own records.

Do not disclose all income. You'll only tempt an unscrupulous lawyer to prolong litigation and inflate fees. It's only necessary for you to show the ability to meet the agreed-upon fee.

If living on welfare, you have immediate access to their legal aid services. If you live within a wage scale below the line established by Legal Aid services, you also have access to their services. Check white pages of phone book to call them.

Insurance for the Family

Insurance is one means God has given man to provide for his household after his death. If He expects a man to care for his family while living, it's reasonable that He expects a man to care for his family when he is dead. Insurance is a way he can do that. And, if he buys *term* insurance (one form of life insurance), he has an excellent way to care for himself and his family now and later. Most people, however, do not have term insurance. They have whole-life.

Whole-life insurance (variously called straight-life, or ordinary-life) is the type of insurance that is told and sold. Eighty-six percent of American people have this kind of life insurance and the reason they have it (rather than term insurance) is because an insurance man *told* them about it. He came *to them* (they didn't go to him) by phone, mail, or in person and sold them a life insurance policy.

Since it was a told-and-sold policy by a life insurance man, rather than a sought-and-bought policy by the consumer, the consumer was not shown the superior advantages of term insurance—which brings in more cash return to the consumer, and is cheaper for the consumer. But, because it brings in less commission for the life insurance salesman, he rarely tells the consumer about it.

With whole-life, the consumer is paying for two things: protection *plus savings*. With all other insurances—fire, home, car and term—you pay only for protection. That's the way it should be. That's what term is.

A life insurance salesman will quickly point out that the savings is a plus. "Sure it's more expensive, but we're investing that additional money for you, accumulating to a nice nest egg when you're 65, and available as savings money to withdraw on anytime you need it. And giving your wife and kids insurance protection the whole time."

There's something they don't say (and, giving them benefit of the doubt, they don't even know perhaps). Take that monthly premium and divide it in half (percentages will vary depending on age, cash value and company). With one-half you can buy the same amount of term-insurance protection. With the other half, you can invest it in your *own* savings program of *your choice* to earn 6%, 8%, or 10% (depending on savings program) instead of the insurance company's 3½%.

Furthermore, if an emergency should arise and you have to borrow from those savings, you do not have to pay interest to the bank to withdraw your own money. A life insurance salesman will assure you that you can withdraw your accumulated cash values *anytime* ("with dividends!," but dearly paid for by higher premiums). But it is not stressed that you will have to pay the insurance company 6% interest. For your own money!

Because of the many disadvantages of whole-life and the clear advantages of term (buying low-cost pure protection and putting the additional money in a savings account), *Consumers Union Report*, 1972, *Let God Manage Your Money* by Gordon MacLean, and *Here's How to Succeed with Your Money* by George Bowman, recommend term insurance.

Compare these charts:

Chart A*

At age 35, a man has $345.40 to spend for insurance. He buys a $20,000 whole-life policy for an annual premium of $345.40. (Remember *total* policy value at any time is $20,000. Cost of this policy: $345.40.)

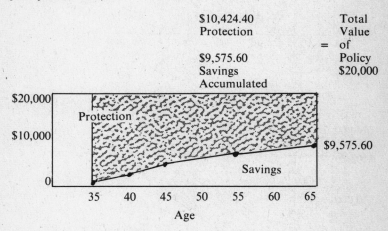

	$10,424.40 Protection		Total Value
		=	of
	$9,575.60 Savings Accumulated		Policy $20,000

At Age	Cash Value is:
35	0
40	779.20
45	2,349.00
55	6,005.40
65	9,575.60

---

*Charts, courtesy of National Institute for Christian Financial Planning.

Chart B

At age 35, a man has $345.40 to spend for insurance. He buys $24,000 of 30-year decreasing term insurance at an annual cost of $93.36. He invests $252.04 annually in two alternate investment vehicles at 6% or 8%.

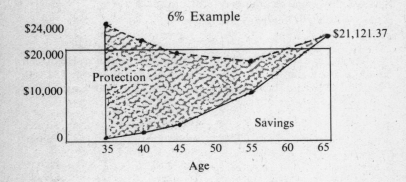

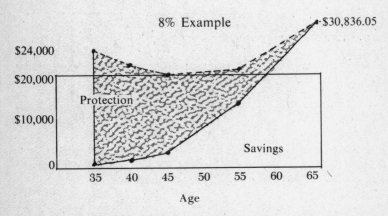

What the charts show is that (Chart A) your protection with whole-life insurance actually *decreases*. ($20,000 worth of protection at age 35; $10,424.40 worth at age 65. At age 65, the policy is still worth $20,000 but $9,575.60 of that is your *own* savings.) Your money in *their* savings ($9,575.60) increases only slightly (at about 3½%).

In other words, at age 65 (for example) you have accumulated $9,575.60 in savings. But if you died then, you (rather, your survivor) would still only get $20,000, $9,575.60 of which is money *you* had saved in the insurance company's 3½% plan. You would be getting, in effect, only $10,424.40 of insurance-protection money.

Chart B shows that if you were to take that same amount of money ($345.40) and invest it in term insurance, you would still maintain adequate coverage and yet be able to earn $21,121.37 (at 6%) or $30,836.05 (at 8%) in a savings plan of your own.

Buy low-cost term insurance and discipline yourself to use the additional money to invest in your own savings plan.

Saving Money on Cars

(1) *Keep speed down.* Tests conducted with one American car indicate a 25 percent improvement in fuel economy when speeds are reduced from 70 to 50 miles per hour. Wind resistance increases as car speed increases, and more energy is thus required to move the car at higher speeds. This is also much safer. Remember, a car (potentially) is a 3,000-pound gun.

(2) *Avoid "Jack Rabbit" starts.* Gradual acceleration in city driving can save as much as two miles per gallon compared to rapid acceleration. That's because it takes a lot of extra energy to increase an automobile's acceleration rate. A power valve, located in the carburetor, lets more fuel into the cylinders under full, quick acceleration.

(3) *Keep speed constant.* Driving at steady speeds helps to save gasoline. Unnecessary acceleration activates the accelerator pump and power valve, thus injecting extra—and wasted—fuel into the system.

(4) *Anticipate stops.* It is best to plan ahead for all traffic conditions, allowing for gradual, rather than abrupt, stops. Smooth driving contributes to better fuel economy and safety.

(5) *Plan all trips.* Plan car trips to cover as many errands as possible at one time. In city driving, a one-mile trip with the engine cold may decrease fuel economy by as much as 70 percent since combustion is relatively inefficient in a cold engine.

(6). *Form car pools.* One of the best ways to conserve gasoline is to form car pools. Motorists can join with friends, neighbors, and co-workers to take one car to a common destination.

(7) *Avoid unnecessary engine idling.* In cold weather, let the

engine idle for 30 seconds before driving off, but never idle excessively; it does no useful work and merely wastes fuel.

(8) *Minimize the use of air conditioners.* Air-conditioning puts a substantial load on automobile engines. While driving at 30 miles per hour, for example, use of the air conditioner can result in a fuel economy loss of two miles per gallon. As a rule, use of the air conditioner cuts gasoline mileage by 10 percent. Also, don't turn on an air conditioner immediately. Drive a little while, windows open, allowing stagnant hot air to blow out. This way, the air conditioner will not have to work as hard to cool the car.

(9) *Keep wheels properly aligned.* When the wheels don't "track" properly, there's a dragging effect on the tires, causing the engine to work harder.

(10) *Maintain correct tire pressure.* Underinflated tires reduce gasoline mileage slightly; soft tires also wear out faster. Tires should not, however, be inflated above the maximum recommended pressure.

(11) *Keep the engine tuned up.* Spark plug misfiring may result in a significant increase in fuel consumption. In addition, ignition timing deviating from the manufacturer's recommended setting decreases fuel economy. These and other obstacles to efficient engine performance can be eliminated with a complete engine tune-up.

What a tune-up includes:

Major Tune-Up (every 10,000 miles)

Install new plugs, ignition points, and condenser.

Clean or replace the positive crankcase ventilating (PCV valve) and remove gum or sludge from the bases.

Check all electrical ignition circuits and connections for voltage drop and resistance. Clean, tighten, and replace them as necessary.

Inspect the choke for proper operation.

Set the timing to the manufacturer's specifications.

Check the ignition advance mechanism (mechanical and vacuum).

Remove foreign matter from the exhaust gas recirculating valve phases, and check the controls following the manufacturer's specifications.

Check the exhaust system for blockage.

Replace air and fuel filter elements.
Check for fuel leaks at carburetor, fuel pump, gas line and gas tank.

Minor Tune-Up

Every 5,000 miles after the major tune-up, a minor tune-up should be performed. This involves cleaning the plugs, and adjusting points and timing as necessary. (Some cars require tune-ups before or after 10,000/5,000 limits. Check owner's manual.)

(12) *Service air filter.* A dirty air filter can cause a decrease in fuel economy, and a decrease in power output, by restricting the flow of air to the engine. Change the air filter at 12,000- or 24,000-mile intervals, according to the manufacturer's recommendations. In addition, frequent air filter servicing is required if considerable driving is done in sandy or dusty conditions. You can change the filter yourself.

(13) *Check the automatic choke.* The automatic choke should be checked regularly, since it regulates the fuel-air mixture. If improperly adjusted, it wastes gasoline.

(14) *Don't ride the brakes..* Even slight foot pressure on the brake pedal can apply the brakes, especially power brakes. This wastes fuel energy which might be used to move the car.

(15) *Keep transmission in high gear.* Keep both automatic and manual transmissions in the highest gear possible. With a manual transmission, shift into high gear as soon as you can; with an automatic transmission, use a light foot on the accelerator to encourage the transmission to shift into high gear quickly.

(16) *Minimize vehicle loads.* Transporting unnecessary weight in your car will cause it to use more fuel. The difference is not great on level ground, but does show up when climbing a hill. You will probably have to use your brakes more often.

(17) *Service the manifold heat control valve.* See that the manifold heat control valve is inspected and serviced at the recommended intervals.

This valve, located in the exhaust system of some cars, allows exhaust gases to heat the intake manifold during cold engine operation.

A valve stuck in the open position causes slow engine warm-up and poor cold-engine performance. A valve stuck in the closed position will cause a loss of power and hard starting with a hot engine. Sticking in either position makes the engine use more fuel.

(18) Shut off motor when at gas station (*safer* and cheaper) and at any extended stop.

(19) Walk to the corner store. Don't drive. Avoid all unnecessary car trips. A standard-sized car costs 14¢ a mile to run.

(20) If you have a safe driving record, you can get lower insurance rates. Check with an insurance broker.

(21) Use gasoline of the proper octane rating. Using too low an octane rating for your car will produce a "ping" which, if sustained, will damage the engine. Using too high an octane rating wastes money and will not produce more power or improve fuel economy.

(22) Use a good quality multi-grade (multi-viscosity) oil having an AP1 SAE rating on the container. Multi-grade low-30 and low-40 oils help reduce internal engine friction and give better gasoline mileage than single grade SAE oils. Do not use an oil of higher viscosity than recommended in your owner's manual since heavier oils tend to increase friction and decrease miles-per-gallon efficiency. A lower viscosity oil such as 5w-30 is recommended for winter months in northern states.

(23) Keep a check on miles per gallon. That's the number of miles you get from one gallon of gas. Record both the amount of gasoline added to your tank at each fill-up and the odometer reading. Miles per gallon is obtained by dividing the miles traveled since the previous fill-up by the gallons added at the last fill-up.

(24) For keeping record of mileage, gas, and all expenses, use Ward's small and handy *Motor Record Book*. It's pocket-size and will help in keeping track of your car expenses. If your local stationary store does not have one, order from John J. Ward, Inc., 23-08 Jackson Avenue, Long Island City, New York 11101.

Buying a Used Car

Study car body for highlights which indicate repainting to (perhaps) hide ripples, bumps, or other signs of sheet metal repair. Find out why the car or sections of the car have been repaired.

Invest $10-$20 in a good mechanic to have him go over the car thoroughly. Also, check with a bank to find out the "Blue Book" price of the used car you are interested in. ("Blue Book" is the standard used-car price list used by car dealers, loan companies, and bankers.)

Check car for rusted-out areas. You'll find these on floor board, underneath car, or on floor of trunk.

Check for worn seats, brake pedal, head rests and arm rests. They are a tell-tale sign that the car has been used heavily.

Check odometer reading by checking mileage on the last couple of oil changes. Oil change stickers should be on car door or car panels. If oil change stickers are missing, find out why. It is illegal for dealers to turn back odometers, but, unfortunately, that doesn't hinder some dealers.

Step down on the brake pedal and hold the pressure steadily for at least 30 seconds. If the pedal continues to sink, even gradually, to the floor, there's a leak in the hydraulic system. Not too serious, but it should be repaired before you buy.

Look under the car for signs of oil leaks. If you find any, get them fixed before purchase.

Start the engine and listen for loud noises and uneven idling when you are starting.

When the engine is thoroughly warmed up, check the exhaust. Is it heavy or blue? If so, it's burning oil. Forget the car.

When you turn off the engine, make sure everything goes off quickly and quietly.

Make sure shock absorbers are not worn out. Rock the car rhythmically at each corner of the car; when you release the car, it should move up and stop at a level position.

Driving tests: Never let the salesman do the driving or select the route. Drive the car yourself under varying road conditions and make the following tests:

Make several starts from rest, both forward and in reverse. An automatic transmission should take hold promptly when placed in gear with no slamming or lurching action. With a manual transmission, feel for clutch slippage.

From a speed of about 15 mph, accelerate the car briskly to about 60 mph. There should be a smooth flow of power with no undue hesitation, knocking, or other strange noises. If there's no smooth flow, look for another car.

Check the steering by making a few sharp turns in both directions. The reaction should be quick and positive without binding.

Make a few brake stops from about 45 mph. The car should stop smoothly without squealing and without fading to the right or left. The brake pedal should feel firm under pressure and rest well above the floor.

Also, use the attached chart as you compare dealers. As you go from dealer to dealer, you won't remember all these details, so *write them down.*

USED CAR BUYING CHECKLIST

	Dealer # 1	Dealer # 2
Make		
Model		
Year		
Body Style		
Inspections		
Body Condition		
Interior		
Gauges/Lights		
Engine		
Brakes		
Tires		
Transmission		
Acceleration		
Steering		
Comments		

Finally, don't accept anything from the salesman—a free lunch, a free pen, a cup of coffee, *nothing.* He'll try to get you to feel obligated to him which, of course, obscures your judgment.

If you plan far enough ahead of time, you can write Car/Puter International Corporation.* For $10 the company tells you what the dealer's cost is and how much he should charge you with a $125 markup.

Buying a New Car

Begin at *home* (not in showroom) to figure what you want in price and accessories. At the showroom, figure cost *first*, *then* drive the car. The salesman, obviously, wants you to drive the car first, hoping you'll like it so much you'll bend during the haggling process.

Financial Marketing Associates says:

> Discounts off the official sticker price are available on most domestic and many imported cars. However, the amount of the discount depends on several factors—time of year, dealer volume, factory incentives, and the price range of the car.
>
> You can determine the approximate dealer cost on any domestic car with a little arithmetic. Take the bottom figure on the official sticker and subtract the transportation charge (also listed on the sticker). Then, for a subcompact or compact, multiply by 0.85. For intermediates, multiply by 0.815. For full-sized cars, multiply by 0.78. To this figure add back the transportation charge, and you will have the dealer's cost within about 1 per cent.
>
> You can't expect the dealer to sell at cost. But with hard bargaining at a high-volume dealership, you may be able to negotiate a minimum markup. Most dealers will accept an offer of 5 to 10 percent over cost. But remember, it's better to make a reasonable deal with a reputable dealer than to save a few dollars by dealing with one with a poor reputation.

Use this chart when comparing cars and dealers:

Dealer _____

Make _____

Model _____

Color _____

---

*1603 Bushwick Ave., Brooklyn, NY 11207.

Options

_____

_____

_____

Price

_____

Trade-in

_____

Difference to Pay

_____

Consider cost of gas before you buy. If you buy a big car, avoid the big V-8's. Considering the Environmental Protection Agency's figures for fuel economy, and assuming a 40-cent gallon, you can easily figure that it costs $1.86 to drive a four-cylinder Vega 100 miles in city traffic, $2.04 for a six-cylinder Valiant, and $4.50 for an eight-cylinder Lincoln. If you do require a big car, specify the *standard* engine rather than a high-powered option. The standard engine will perform adequately and save fuel.

Protecting Your Car (And Your Life) From Hidden Defects

Evelyn Kantor says:

Since 1973, 8.9 million vehicles have been recalled for defects ranging from split safety-belt anchorings to potentially unsafe power-braking systems, but millions of possibly hazardous cars remain on the road because their owners either did not receive recall notices or ignored them. The National Highway Traffic Safety Administration will tell you whether your model has been recalled, and provide you with information on any recall campaigns that have involved your model, including the date and number of the recall campaign and the reason for the recall—vital information when (or after) buying a used car. The NHTSA will also send you a form to send to the manufacturer to authorize a repair if necessary.

Armed with this information and your Vehicle Identification Number, contact either the dealer or the manufacturer, who should be able to tell you if the defect has been repaired. If it has not, send the form to the manufacturer to have a repair authorized. Contact Office of Consumer Services, NHTSA: 400 7th St. SW; Washington, D.C. 20590 (202 426-0670).[19]

Car Repair

Before running to repair shop, check car yourself first. Don't run to buy a new battery simply because your car won't start. Maybe the battery cable is off the terminals or terminals are corroded. All it takes is putting the cable snugly on the terminals or scraping the terminals. Takes a minute and costs nothing.

One woman ran to the telephone because her "transmission had fallen out"—the clanging, banging and scraping sounded like it. A peek under the car revealed that the tail pipe had dropped, which required a piece of shoestring to tie it to the frame until she got home where her husband replaced the necessary bolts.

Carry in your car an emergency repair kit. This includes jumper cables, flashlight, siphon pump, distress flags, flares, duct tape, wire, paper clips, tire inflator, plastic water bag, screwdrivers, adjustable wrench. Investment in a repair kit *now* may prevent not only night-time isolation out in nowhere, but also a costly road call and towing charge.

Check it our yourself first. You save hundreds of dollars by doing simple repair jobs yourself:

Air filter. This rests inside that round container that looks like a covered cake pan on top of the engine. The cover is generally held on with wing nuts or clamps that come off easily. Lift out the filter and take a look at it. Most are the paper throwaway type. If it is clearly dirty, buy a replacement at prices ranging from about $1.50 to $3.00.

Fuses. When one or more of the electrical appliances on your car refuses to work, the cause may be a burned-out fuse. Manufacturers often hide fuse boxes under the dash, so if your owner's manual doesn't tell you where it is, check with the man at the gas station. Knowing the location and having a spare set of fuses and a fuse puller—total cost about $1.25—can be very handy in an emergency.

Tail and backup lights. On some models you must unscrew the lens covering to replace a burned-out bulb, but on many you just reach inside the trunk, grasp the rubber fitting and twist it either right or left, so that the bulb and socket pull free. Twist the old bulb out and put the new one in the same way. Bulbs cost less than $1 a pair.

Minor lubrication. You can get rid of many of your car's annoying squeaks and rattles and even make some parts work better by doing a little lubrication. A can of silicone spray for about a dollar will work wonders on hinges and catches. Powdered graphite will make door locks work smoothly. Automatic-choke cleaner will help your carburetor work smoothly if you follow the directions on the spray can.

Fluid checks. Periodic checks of the fluid levels in the power steering, automatic transmission and brake master cylinder can save a lot of grief. Your owner's manual should tell you where these are, or you may have to search a bit.

The power steering pump is at the front of the engine. Unscrew the top, check the dipstick, and if the level is low and the steering has been making growling noises, you should add fluid.

The automatic transmission dipstick (at the rear of the engine) looks like the engine oil dipstick and has the same "add" and "full" marks on it. Check the transmission fluid level with the engine running at an idle, car in "park" on level ground. You need an inexpensive tool to add this fluid—a funnel with a tube on the end to get the fluid into the tube where the dipstick rests.

The master cylinder is located near the rear of the engine compartment. Wipe all dirt away from the edges of the cover and take it off; many covers are held with a wire clamp, some have a screw top. Fluid should be within a quarter to a half inch of the top. The owner's manual will tell you which types of fluid to use. Do not overfill any of the components.

Headlights. Replacing a burned-out lamp merely involves buying the right size and taking out a few screws from the trim ring covering the light. You then will see the headlight held in place by a metal retainer ring that usually is secured by three screws. Loosen these and rotate the ring counter-clockwise so that you can lift it off. Don't touch the aiming screws or you will have to get the aim readjusted. As you lift out the lamp, you will see that it is plugged into a socket. Unplug the old, plug in the new and reverse your work procedure to put everything back in place. On some cars, those made by General Motors, for instance, the rings are held by springs, which usually can be disengaged with a hook made of coat hanger wire or with a pair of needle nose pliers.

Gas filter. A dirty filter can stop your car from running and mean an expensive trouble call. A new one costs only a dollar or so. Many are in plain sight—a little container clamped into the fuel line running to the carburetor. Some require a brief but worthwhile search. Loosen the clamps and pull out the old filter.

This may take some tugging and a little gas may spill, but you can wipe it up later. Install the new filter in the same direction as the old one and make sure the clamps are tight.

PCV valve. A dirty Positive Crankcase Ventilation valve can cause plenty of engine problems. A new one costs about a dollar or two, and once you find its location in your engine, it's quickly installed. On four- or six-cylinder engines the PCV valve is usually stuck at the end of a rubber tube that emerges from a rubber fitting atop the valve cover. On V-8's it is often at the end of a tube emerging from the intake manifold, the casting on which the carburetor sits. Some are held by a clip or clamp, others will come out with just a sharp tug. If the tubing appears gummy inside, you should remove it and clean it by running a piece of heavy wire and kerosene through it. Let it dry and replace everything.

Checking and replacing coolant. For a couple of dollars you can buy a four-ball hydrometer, a gadget that measures the strength of your radiator's coolant. Follow the directions on the box, and take the worry out of winter freeze-ups. You can buy antifreeze at sales and add it as your check-ups show it's needed. And it is far cheaper and often more prudent than waiting until you can get to a gas station.

Replacing hoses. A radiator hose that appears cracked or brittle is existing on borrowed time. You may need a flashlight to see those at the bottom of the engine. To replace a top radiator hose, put a drain pan under the radiator, open the jetcock at the bottom with pliers and run off enough coolant to lower the level below the hose. To replace the bottom hose, you must drain all the coolant. If it is still fresh, you can pour it back when you finish.

Take the clamps off the hose and pry the hose off the connecting necks with a screwdriver. Make sure the necks are clean and then slide the new hose on. You can use a thin coat of sealing compound on the necks, but a good clamp usually will hold the hose tightly enough. Buy the metal-band type that tightens with a screw at about 50 cents a pair. Hoses average $1.50 to $2.00. If the system is dirty and needs flushing, buy a can of radiator flush.

Battery care. Take off the caps on your battery and look inside. Water should just reach the filler rings. You may need a flashlight to see properly. *Never use a match.* Unless the local water has a lot of iron in it, you can safely use tap water, although many people prefer to stick with distilled. A plastic squeeze bottle allows neat, quick filling.

The terminal posts should be kept clean. You can remove some of the white deposits with a wire brush, then cover them with a paste of baking soda and water. While this is eating away the deposits, stick toothpicks temporarily in the vent holes on the cell caps, if there are any, so you can wash the mess away with clean water without getting any inside the battery. You can also pull the cable clamps from the terminal posts and scour the inside of the clamps and the terminal posts with a piece of emery paper. Put them back so tightly that you can't move them, and coat the terminals and cable clamps with a nonmetallic grease. Vaseline works well. If the cables are corroded, you can replace them for $1.00 apiece. A terminal lifter tool, for about $3.50, simplifies the job.

Fan and other belts. Every 5,000 to 6,000 miles you should check the belts that run the fan, power steering and air-conditioning. *The engine must be off when you do this.* A loose fan belt can cause over-heating; a loose power steering belt can cause an annoying squeal when you turn the wheel. You can test the tension by pressing hard on the belt with your thumb midway between pulleys. The belt should deflect about half an inch if the center-to-center distance between pulleys is 13 to 16 inches. It should deflect a quarter of an inch if the distance is 7 to 10 inches. A more precise method is to use a belt tension gauge, but these are relatively expensive.

Adjusting the tension is not too difficult in many cases. Loosen the holding bolts of the component involved— alternator, power steering pump or the idler pulley for the air conditioner. Using a pry bar, press the component back to firm up the tension. Tighten the bolts and check the tension. When adjusting the fan belt, press only against the center of the alternator. Pressing on the back portion of the casing may cause damage. Frayed or cracked belts should be replaced—about $1.50 apiece. New belts will stretch a bit almost immediately, so recheck the tension after idling the engine for several minutes. Do not over-tighten the belts; this could strain and damage components.

Oil and filter change. This is seldom a neat job, but it is not difficult. Buying at sales, you can often find a good-quality

Pennsylvania base oil at prices as low as 50 cents a quart. Filters may be less than $2. You'll also need a wrench to take out the drain bolt on the oil pan and a pan to catch the old oil. For the common screw-on type of oil filter you'll need a filter wrench, which costs less than $2.

Park on a level spot, run the engine briefly to warm the oil, then turn it off and make sure the car is securely braced and braked. Crawl underneath to loosen the drain plug. Have the pan ready to catch the oil and make the final turns with your fingers. Try to keep your arm up and out of the way. When the oil has drained, use your filter wrench to loosen the filter. Drain the old oil from it and throw the filter away. Put the old oil into plastic milk jugs and take it to a gas station for disposal.

Put the drain plug back tightly and with a clean cloth, wipe the area where the filter fits. With your finger, spread some new engine oil around the gasket of the new filter and screw it on hand tight. Do not use the filter wrench. You can use a cheap funnel to pour the oil into the filler neck; your owner's manual will tell you how much. Run the engine for about five minutes, turn off the engine and check underneath for leaks. Then pull out the dipstick to check the oil level. Remember that a new filter soaks up about a quart of oil.

Tune-ups. As you gain confidence, you may be tempted to try a complete tune-up on your car. You can learn how in various ways. Many courses are offered through high school adult education programs, community colleges and even some auto dealerships. Chrysler, for example, has a Women on Wheels program that is conducted all over the country. That one is for women only, but at most courses both men and women are welcome and attend in about equal numbers.

Check the public library or a bookstore for auto repair books. Three popular ones: *How to Service and Repair Your Own Car* by Richard Day (Popular Science, $10.95); *Auto Repairs You Can Make* by Paul Weissler (Arco, $6.95); and *Repair Your Own Car for Pennies . . . It's Easy* by Arthur Darack (Consumers Digest, $1.95).

Don't overlook your owner's manual. Many have helpful maintenance and repair sections—American Motors and Chevrolet Vega, for example. Ford offers special light-repair manuals aimed at beginners for almost all its models from 1971 on at $2.25 each. Experts can order complete factory manuals from the manufacturers, but understanding these requires a lot of basic knowledge.

And don't be afraid to ask a neighbor to help. People are dying to feel useful. If he can help you with your car, you're doing *him* a favor.

When you do take your car to a shop to be repaired (or simply pull into an unfamiliar gas station for gas), you're a potential target for an unscrupulous attendant.

You might learn, for example, says *Changing Times*, that your gas cap is "missing." The attendant sells you one and later sells yours to another unsuspecting motorist. Or you find that your oil is a quart low. It appears so because the attendant has "short-sticked" you by not pushing the dipstick all the way into the crankcase. He can perform his sleight of hand even while you are standing there by tilting the stick a bit so that its cap hits the edge of the hole, making a clicking sound, just as if the stick had been seated properly.

He might then actually put in a quart of oil you don't need (which isn't good for the motor) or he can pretend to put it in by using an empty container. He makes the empty can look like a full one by putting the oil spout into the unused end and holding a rag over the end with a hole in it.

One of the most common ploys is to get you to buy unneeded repairs when your car begins acting up on a trip. If you've been having starting difficulty, you can easily be sold a new battery when the trouble might just be vapor lock caused by the hot weather and hot engine. A cold, wet rag on the fuel line and pump could have solved the problem.

Or suppose your car's engine begins missing suddenly after you have accelerated past a slow-moving truck. You pull worriedly into a staion, where the mechanic listens briefly to the motor and says that you need a complete tune-up, including new spark plug wires. Maybe you do, but he can't tell for sure with such a cursory examination. Perhaps the miss was caused by a fleck of carbon lodged between the electrodes of a spark plug. And perhaps the only immediate repair needed is to push out the carbon and replace the plug. (Spark plug wires usually last about 25,000 miles, and most cars will run 12,000 to 15,000 miles between tuneups.) If your trouble was a stuttering engine, you might also be sold anything from a new fuel pump to a new carburetor, along with a new fuel filter, when all you needed was the filter.

Some of the wilder frauds are worked when you step away from the car to buy a soft drink or visit the restroom. That's when a greedy operator has ample opportunity to pull one or more wires loose so that the car won't start or the trouble lights go on. On some models, for example, you can disconnect one small, unobtrusive wire and the car will start but die immediately. You're a mark then for the sale of a new alternator, voltage regulator, coil or whatever else the operator has in mind. He might cut a fan belt or hose or puncture a tire, then point out the trouble with a glum face. Some have been known to squirt oil on a shock absorber to make it appear to be leaking. Because shocks must be installed in pairs, he has you for an expensive repair bill. To compound the injury, he might not even replace them, but merely clean off the old ones so they look like new.

Some technically minded bandits spray titanium tetra-chloride—a colorless liquid that creates dense white smoke—onto the alternator to scare the wits and the money out of the unsuspecting motorist. Others put soda into batteries to make them foam.

They can cheat you without getting their hands dirty by "kiting" your credit card invoice. One way is to use your card to print a second invoice, which the crook fills in later. If you notice the forgery, you don't have to pay, of course. But some credit card billings don't include gasoline invoices, and many motorists neglect to save them. Another technique is to set the credit card printer to show a different figure from the handwritten total. The operator can then alter the handwritten number after you leave. To discourage this, many credit card companies now note on their invoices that both totals must agree and have printed red arrows pointing from one to the other.

You can end up on the losing end of a monumental gyp right in your own neighborhood. You usually find different types of gyps and deceptions at different types of facilities, but the boundaries aren't particularly rigid.

Gas stations and garages. It's unlikely that the gas station or garage that normally services your car would gyp you. The mechanic might make a mistake, but who doesn't occasionally? Or he might install a part or two that you don't need right this minute because he knows through experience that you will need those parts in a couple of months and he won't see you again for six.

But at a place where they don't know you and doubt that

they'll ever see you again, an attendant might short-stick you, sell you an air cleaner to replace one that's perfectly clean or talk you into buying a can of gasoline additive that is supposed to, but won't, stop your engine from stumbling. Only a good mechanic can cure that.

Dealerships. The service departments of many new-car dealerships are constantly struggling to break even or make a profit, which means that you might be singled out for special attention when your car coughs its way into a service bay. You ask for a tune-up and routine service checks and before you know it you've got a bill that includes the usual tune-up parts, oil and filter, new hoses and belts, labor charges for various adjustments and for repacking the front wheel bearings—a total cost of $100 or more. Maybe you needed all that work. Okay. But you should ask in advance what you are likely to have to pay for.

The plain fact is that some dealerships routinely pour a can of unnecessary additive into the oil, replace some parts simply because their parts inventory is too high and charge a substantial amount on each bill for "shop materials" (a dab of grease here, a spot of lubricant there). Parts replacement helps the mechanic do the job more quickly because replacing a string of parts is easier than figuring out which one is faulty.

Some states that require periodic safety inspection of vehicles allow the inspection stations to do repairs. Other states, Ohio for example, have *state* inspection stations. They do no repairs but only show you repairs your car needs to pass state inspection level. You then go to your own mechanic. If your state does not have state inspection stations, ask your state representative to introduce a bill to that effect.

Although the stations are policed, it's particularly difficult to catch the ones who require unneeded repairs because some car owners simply accept the practice and many others never realize they've been had. The cheaters have a tendency to adjust headlights that need no adjustment and to replace idler arms—a section of the steering linkage—that really are fine as is. Occasionally, one will present a huge list of repairs—new suspension parts, tires, gas tank. Any sensible motorist will immediately check with another mechanic to find out what really does need fixing.

Franchisers and mass merchandisers. It's easy to fall prey to the come-ons of places that specialize in certain kinds of repairs because the prices appear to be such a bargain. Even if you read some of the ads several times, however, it can be tough to figure out just what it is that they give you for that low price—a situation that the Federal Trade Commission is watching closely these days.

Typically, a front-end alignment is offered at a very small price, as low as $4.95, or even free in some cases. It's not only unlikely that you'll get a good alignment for that kind of money—a quality shop might charge three times as much—but you can be laying yourself open to a variety of hustles, like those described earlier.

The best single thing you can do to assure good service at fair prices is to devote some time to finding a good shop. Seek out acquaintances who are knowledgeable about cars and ask where they have their work done. You may find that a highly recommended shop is inconveniently located. Going out of your way to get the work done right is worth it.

Tell the owner who recommended him and indicate that you would like to have him take care of your car from now on. If the shop doesn't do some types of repair, such as alignment and heavy transmission work, the mechanics can probably recommend good places that do.

To protect yourself, keep these points in mind:

Make sure that your car is in good condition before you set out on a trip.

Don't leave the car unattended at a strange station. Get out and watch what the attendant is doing. If you must leave the car to visit the rest room or snack bar, park and lock it.

Don't ignore early trouble symptoms—odd noises from the engine, poor acceleration—until it's too late. Pull in while you still have some mobility. Then if you hear an unlikely tale, you can limp down the road to another shop.

If you don't know a coil from a carburetor, be quiet about your ignorance. Broadcasting your lack of knowledge could be an open invitation to a good fleecing.

If you do feel you've been taken at a gas station, write to the president of the oil company and local Chamber of Commerce. If you are a member of AAA (or similar auto club) and have a complaint against one of their bonded stations, you have recourse through that organization.

Several states—California, Connecticut, Massachusetts,

Washington, D.C.—and many cities and counties currently license repair garages so that if chicanery is found the culprits can be prosecuted. Some 32 other states and at least 40 jurisdictions are considering some form of licensing. Further, many states have consumer protection offices to which you can direct your complaint, or you can write directly to the state prosecutor's office, which has the legal clout to deal with fraud.

Getting Out of Debt, Staying Out of Debt

A Chicago woman wrote to a financial counselor:

> Please help us to get off the financial merry-go-round we've been on for the ten years we've been married. Our problem is and always has been debts that are practically impossible to pay but must be paid. To do so we rob Peter to pay Paul and so have never really paid any of them. We've simply shifted the load from one finance company to another. When we got married my husband was making $40 a week and was in debt. We still are, though he now makes $175 a week. With our four children came much happiness, many doctor and hospital bills, the responsibilities and again debts of establishing and furnishing a home. This was done on the installment plan, and when the pinch was tight, back to the finance company again. Surely, there is an answer, but it is evading us completely.

It is easy to get in debt these days; the trick is to find an easy way to get out. It's easy to spend impulsively; the trick is to save impulsively.

Because of the ease of sliding into debt, family indebtedness increased 40% during the last decade, *in the middle of an economic boon.*

Indebtedness has definite causes and definite cures.

Causes: High on the list as a debt-producing culprit is the ubiquitous credit card.

The University of Michigan's Institute for Social Research discovered the following:

> Some 50 percent of all American families use credit cards. As a rule, the higher a household's income the more likely that at least one member will own a credit card. Of families with annual incomes above $20,000, more than four out of five have a member with a plastic-packed wallet.
>
> Clothing is the credit-card user's favorite purchase, made most often with a department-store credit card. Cards issued by

"I *gave* you all my credit cards. Now let me have the car keys." [20]

individual or chains of stores are used to make more purchases of all kinds than any other cards. Of the individuals who carry store-issued cards, 90 percent use them to purchase clothing. More than three out of five people who have bank cards also use them at clothing stores.

Three quarters of all American families—including those that don't use credit cards—feel that the plastic substitutes for money tempt one to buy more than is necessary.

The west is the credit-card center of the U.S. Some 67 percent of all western families use credit cards compared with 52 percent of north central area families, 48 percent of northeastern area families, and 42 percent of southern families.

Suburbanites carry more plastic money than central-city dwellers or those living beyond the suburban rings around major cities. More than 70 percent of all suburbanites carry credit cards compared with 43 percent of central-city dwellers and 37 percent of outlying-area residents.

The most frequent user of credit cards is the man under 45 who has young children. Sixty-five percent of the fathers in this age bracket who have children at least six years old use credit cards. Some 58 percent of fathers over 45 use the cards.

Most credit cards surface from the depths of their owners' wallets at least once a month. Of people carrying at least one card, four out of five use it at least once a month or more.

The American car's thirst for gasoline makes a significant

contribution to the overall frequency of credit-card use. More than 80 percent of gasoline-credit-card holders buy fuel at least once a month with their oil cards. After store and gasoline cards, the next most frequently used cards are issued by banks. Some 55 percent of the holders of bank cards use them to make a monthly purchase.

The average card holder's bill for one month's purchase on his credit cards is between $50.00 and $75.00. One out of every five credit card users runs up a monthly bill of more than $1,000.00, while 8 percent make total credit-card purchases of more than $200.00 a month.

The wallet of the average credit-card holder contains three. Some 14 percent of all card holders stuff their wallets with six, while 8 percent have sagging pockets from carrying nine or more. The cards duplicated most frequently in wallets and purses are those issued by department stores and oil companies.

The survey reports that credit-card use is not having the anticipated effect on the way card holders manage their checking accounts.

Families using credit cards were expected to reduce the number of checks they wrote each month because several purchases could be made with one card and paid for with a single check to the issuer of the credit card. However, the institute found families using credit cards write one or two more checks a month than other families with identical incomes who don't use credit cards.*

Any questions about why you should tear up your credit card? It costs 18% to use a credit card, by the way. Using a credit card to buy a $100 suit means the suit costs $118, plus the bother of another bill to pay at month's end and the harassment of the company if you are late.

If you have a billfold stuffed with credit cards, you have a skull stuffed with mush.

"Keeping up with the Jones" is a common reason people fall into relentless indebtedness. A Milwaukee man suggested to his wife that they reduce their spending on entertainment. He also wanted his wife to get drapes for their new house. But she was immobilized about the choice after getting an estimate of $1,800 for drapes for the living and dining rooms alone. The husband felt she was refusing to face the reality of their income—$15,000—for a family of four. But she wouldn't settle for less

---

*David C. Cook, "Credit Cards Blamed for Impulsive Buying," *Christian Science Monitor*, quoted in Houston Post, October 1, 1972, pp. 1 ff.

than what her friends had. The underlying problem was her own low self-esteem. She could not feel secure unless she had everything that Jones had.

Closely related to that is *greed*. What we see, we want. What we see a lot of, we want a lot of. And since Madison Avenue puts a lot of gadgets and goodies before our eyes (many "on the installment plan"), we lust a lot. An antidote to greed, other than sheer self-discipline, is *giving*. When you give money away (to worthy individuals and charities, of course), you find two things happen: (1) You discover a power over money. You discover that you control it, it doesn't control you. And (2) You discover more money available to you. The more you give, the more you get—from sources you never dreamed about.

Another cause is lack of family planning and purpose. A definite and shared system for handling the family money is important along with a shared spending plan. Dr. Milton Haber's survey of 100 overindebted couples in Michigan found a lack of understanding or agreement on responsibility for handling money. Nearly a third of the couples couldn't agree who was responsible for the debts. In contrast, among other couples who were *not* in debt, interveners found clear communication on who paid the bills, kept the budget, and so on.

When You Have to Borrow

Credit is a good servant but a bad master. Avoid it. There are, however, one or two necessary uses of credit. A crisis may compel you to borrow cash. A young family may need credit to buy certain appliances that could actually save them money.

If you must borrow or buy on credit, here is how you can keep your costs to a minimum:

(1) *Compare the true annual interest rates.* By law, lenders and installment sellers must state in their contracts the annual percentage rate they charge on credit plans, as well as the dollar cost. Orally, however, a lender or salesperson may merely state the monthly rate or the dollar cost per $100 of original loan. These methods of stating finance charges make them sound much cheaper than they really are. Thus, it is vital to ask beforehand the annual percentage rate. This annual rate gives you a yardstick for comparing finance charges among different sources of credit. Without it, you will have difficulty comparing such charges.

(2) *Shop for the lowest rate.* Listed below are typical charges

of different places from which you can get a loan or buy on credit.

Credit unions charge a maximum of 1 percent a month on the declining balance. This is the equivalent of a true annual rate of 12 percent. If you borrowed $100 from a credit union, to be repaid in installments, your dollar cost would be $6.50 a year. You often can borrow cash from a credit union to buy big items for less than a dealer's or finance company's credit charges.

Credit unions generally are sponsored by labor unions, employers, churches, lodges, housing developments, and other groups. Some are organized on a community-wide basis. If you don't belong to one, you can write to the Credit Union National Association, P.O. Box 431, Madison, Wisconsin 53701, for the address of your state credit union league. In turn it can tell you whether there is a credit union for which you are eligible. You also can get a booklet, "How to Organize a Credit Union," from your labor union or from the AFL-CIO Department of Publications, 815 - 16th Street, N.W., Washington, D.C. 20006.

Commerical banks are another reasonable source for small loans. They generally charge "discount" rates of $6 to $8 a year per $100 of the original amount borrowed. These are true rates of approximately 12 to 16 percent a year. But on "ready cash" and credit-card plans, banks charge more: true annual rates of 15 to 18 percent.

Warning: Some people think that the mere fact that a bank allows them to borrow money proves that they are in solid financial shape and need not worry too much about their financial state. Banks, after all, only loan money on a "sure thing." False.

When the money market is sluggish, banks have a tendency to bend the rules a little bit on who qualifies for a loan. They may allow you to borrow more than you can really afford, pointing out that only *you* can discipline yourself.

Department stores and mail-order houses generally charge 1 ½ per cent a month on the declining balance—true rates of 18 percent a year, or $9.75 on a debt of $100.

Installment dealers charge widely varying rates. The most scrupulous ones may charge $10 a year per $100 of debt. This is an annual percentage rate of approximately 20 percent. Others may charge more. But in every case you need to compare the price of each carefully.

Credit card. If you've kept your credit card (despite what I

said earlier), you can borrow on it—if you want to pay 18%
interest.

Loan companies. If you want *more* than 18% interest, and in-
vite the possibility of harassing phone calls to you, your mother,
brother, cousin, or father-in-law (to find out why *you're* late in
payment), then go to a loan company for money.

The chart below gives an example of what it costs to borrow
money for purchases. The chart shows that under one schedule
with $600 in purchases as a starting balance, and no new
purchases added, you'd be in debt for nearly three and a half
years, and finance charges *would cost you over $100*, almost one-
fifth as much as *the purchases themselves.*

Date	Balance	Minimum Payment		Finance Charge	Payment on Principal
1/1	$600.00	$ 60.00		$ .00	$ 60.00
2/1	540.00	54.00	(1 %)	5.40	48.60
3/1	491.40	40.00	(1.5%)	7.37	32.63
4/1	458.77	40.00		6.88	33.12
5/1	425.65	35.00		6.39	28.61
6/1	397.04	30.00		5.96	24.04
7/1	373.00	30.00		5.60	24.40
8/1	348.60	25.00		5.23	19.77
9/1	328.83	25.00		4.93	20.07
10/1	308.76	25.00		4.63	20.37
11/1	288.39	20.00		4.33	15.67
12/1	272.72	20.00		4.09	15.91
1/1	256.81	20.00		3.85	16.15
2/1	240.66	15.00		3.61	11.39
3/1	229.27	15.00		3.44	11.56
4/1	217.71	15.00		3.27	11.73
5/1	205.98	15.00		3.09	11.91
6/1	194.07	10.00		2.91	7.09
7/1	186.98	10.00		2.80	7.20
8/1	179.78	10.00		2.70	7.30
9/1	172.48	10.00		2.59	7.41
10/1	165.07	10.00		2.49	7.51
11/1	157.56	10.00		2.36	7.64
12/1	149.92	10.00		2.25	7.75
1/1	142.17	10.00		2.13	7.87
2/1	134.30	10.00		2.02	7.98
3/1	126.32	10.00		1.89	8.11
4/1	118.21	10.00		1.77	8.23
5/1	109.98	10.00		1.65	8.35
6/1	101.63	10.00		1.52	8.48
7/1	93.15	10.00		1.40	8.60

8/1	84.55	10.00	1.27	8.73
9/1	75.82	10.00	1.14	8.86
	66.96	10.00	1.00	9.00
11/1	57.96	10.00	.87	9.13
12/1	48.83	10.00	.73	9.27
1/1	39.56	10.00	.59	9.41
2/1	30.15	10.00	.50	9.50
3/1	20.65	10.00	.50	9.50
4/1	11.15	10.00	.50	9.50
5/1	1.65	2.15	.50	1.65
41 mos.		$716.15	$116.15	$600.00

When You Can't Meet Payments

Get in touch with creditors immediately. Explain why payments may be late and how much you expect to pay each week or month that follows. If possible, send a check (regardless of how small) with your letter of explanation. Creditors like it if you call them before they call you. If you delay contacting creditors, however, until payments are overdue, they become worried and less receptive to arrangements you suggest.

Note, however, that you have protection against creditors who harass and threaten. Effective March 20, 1978, the Fair Debt Collection Practices Acts stipulates that

   (a) A collector may not make contact with a debtor at inconvenient times or places—like at work, or at 3 a.m.
   (b) Within 5 days after the collector makes contact with a debtor, the debtor has the right to a written notice from the collector explaining exactly how much is owed, to whom, and what the debtor can do if he thinks it is not accurate.
   (c) A collector may not imply that he is a lawyer or represents an arm of the goverment. He may not accuse the debtor of committing a crime if he actually hasn't.
   (d) A collector may not say that a debtor will be imprisoned if the bill isn't paid. Nor may he say that the debtor's property or paycheck is subject to garnishment—unless the creditor actually intends to do so.

(To issue a complaint or for further information, write Federal Trade Commission, Debt Collection Practices, Wash., D.C. 20580.)

Don't run to another loan company, hoping to borrow more money to pay off the first. The robbing-Peter-to-pay-Paul syndrome leads to a crackup.

You may need financial counseling. A full-service and excellent financial counseling service is *The National Institute for Christian Financial Planning.* (You need not be a Christian to use the service.) If there is not a local representative in your community, you may write them at their national headquarters, 1435 Highland Ave., Melbourne, Fla. 32935. They will get in touch with the representative closest to you.

Headed by veteran businessmen, professional accountants, and trained counselors, they are truly a *service* organization. They have helped the very rich to wisely invest their abundance, the very poor to keep going on the little they have, and the middle-class to discipline spending and build a hedge against inflation. If there are personal, marriage, or family problems contributing to your financial problems, they help with that too.

Here's what you can expect when you call them: First, you'll be asked to fill out a form giving such facts as the number of people in your family, ages, take-home pay, other income and so on, and then with the help of the counselor you will complete a detailed list of your expenses: contributions, housing, food, auto, insurance, medical, clothing, personal expenditures, entertainment, gifts, education, payroll deductions and any miscellaneous costs. Each of these categories is broken down further. Under housing, for example, there are lines for rent or mortgage payment, money spent on each utility, taxes and so on. Under personal expenses you'll put down such things as money spent at barber and beauty shops, and for allowances, coffee-breaks, toiletries. You will also list your debts—the amount owed each creditor, monthly payments, reason for the debt and any delinquencies in payments.

As you go over the expenses, the counselor will probe for weak spots and suggest ways, large and small, to get more for your money. He may warn that you are renting or buying more expensive housing than you can afford. Your food budget will be compared with what other families in similar circumstances spend, and the counselor may point out ways to trim it. Your will and insurance programs will get close scrutiny.

He may point out that your will is vague or needs to be updated. If you don't have a will, he will insist that you get one and will help you to do so. In pointing out the necessity of a will, he may share with you the insights of the Marshall family who learned the hard way the value of a will after Mr. Marshall died. Mrs. Peter Marshall said:

> Apparently he (Mr. Marshall) had thought that since he possessed little other than insurance, making me the sole beneficiary, that took care of the situation. If only he had known how much it left to be taken care of! Yet in thinking a will unimportant for those with a small or moderate estate, my husband was not unusual. I learned later that an estimated 70% of American property owners die intestate.
>
> The first business complication developed when Peter's check account (we did not have a joint one) was frozen. Consequently, no money could be drawn out even for funeral expenses or immediate needs. All of the insurance policies were in a strong box at the bank. That box was immediately sealed by the bank under the Internal Revenue Department's regulations. It took three weeks of cutting red tape before even the insurance agent could get into the strong box "to initiate the collection of death proceeds" as the insurance term has it.
>
> Then I learned that . . . when a man dies without a will, after all the debts are paid, his widow receives one-third of his estate, his child or children, two-thirds. It was necessary for me to appear in probate court to post an expensive bond and to be made administratrix of Peter's affairs. Everything thereafter came under the jurisdiction of this court. Not even funeral expenses, doctor or hospital bills, nor ordinary household expenses could be paid until the court passed on them.
>
> . . . .
>
> Then came the day when I had to reappear in probate court to be made Peter John's guardian. Since then, I have been required to give a detailed financial accounting of my guardianship to the court each year. This will go on until my son becomes of age. Each year the account figures must be sworn to before a notary public. Each year a fee must be paid to the office of Registrar of Wills for the accounting.
>
> When I discovered the amazing amount of red tape involved even with such a small estate, I almost ran to a lawyer to get help in making a will of my own. Not only that, but I began urging my parents and friends to consider the same move. Though in my case there was little to leave anyone, I reasoned that the tiny sum involved in making a will might some day save many times that amount in fees for dealing with quite unnecessary legal technicalities.[21]

He may find that you are paying premiums on health insurance even though you have duplicate coverage through your employer as well as medical insurance that is part of your auto or home-owners policy. He may find that you are strapped to expensive whole-life insurance. If you are, he'll show you how to take out term insurance and put the balance in savings.

The counselor will question you about your major financial goals. He'll show you what resources you can now draw on, how much more you'll need to reach your goals and how to go about accumulating the necessary funds.

If your immediate worry is a stack of unpaid bills that you don't know how you're going to pay, the counselor will help you cut expenses to the bone so you can. If that doesn't do the trick, he'll probably advise you to let the counseling service "prorate" your debts, that is, pay them off in a scheduled way that is fair to each creditor. To do this, he'll get your creditors to agree to let you spread payments over a longer period of time at reduced monthly rates without piling on additional finance charges. In tough cases the creditors might be urged to forgive some of the interest charges or even reduce the debt by a bit. In any case, you get the relief of getting creditors off your back.

If there's no way you can get debts off your back (i.e., if you're irreversibly in debt), the counselor will guide through the painful—but often welcome—procedure of bankruptcy. Bankruptcy simply means two things: (a) financially, you have a clean slate—you can start all over again; and (b) you will not be allowed to buy on credit for seven years. (And if you start buying on credit *again* after the seven-year limit, you've got rocks between your ears.)

Remember, bankruptcy *legally* relieves you of debt. If you feel morally obligated to repay the debts, you may still do so later when you have been able to catch up—without pressure from creditors.

For the counselor's services, you will be charged a nominal fee. And you will not be turned away if you cannot afford the fee. Furthermore, as a Christian, you will put worry in its place. The Bible says: "Trust in the Lord with all your heart, and do not rely on your own insight" (Prov. 3:5, RSV). "I have been young, and now am old; yet I have not seen the righteous forsaken, or his children begging bread" (Ps. 37:25, RSV).

Saving Money Here 'n There

(1) Form a baby-sitting club in your neighborhood, saving the cost of a baby-sitter.

(2) Buy a thermos and put your own coffee in it for work. Restaurant coffee now runs 36¢ to 60¢ a cup. For the cost of a few cups, you can get a good thermos and carry good home-brewed coffee.

(3) Buying lunch is a loser. For the $2 to $4 it costs, you can buy a couple of loaves of bread plus jelly, peanut butter, meat, cheese and/or tomatoes to last for a week of sandwiches for lunch.

(4) When moving, don't hire the first You-Haul-It-Yourself van. Check around. Rental trucks and trailer prices are competitive. (Also, when moving, call one of the many apartment-hunting agencies in your "new" city. Their services are usually free.)

(5) Good grief, hold a garage sale! What's obsolete or plain junk to you is quaint and useful to another. Clothes (especially children's), toys, bottles, books, jewelry, sporting gear—drag them out, fix them up, tag them ridiculously low and they will sell.

(6) When you need an item that you will use only once or twice, like a power saw, rug shampooer, or party items, *rent*, don't buy.

(7) Don't buy a TV. Since most TV is at least inane and at worst harmful, you don't need the expense and danger of having one around the house. When something worthwhile is showing, rent one.

(8) If vinyl covered kitchen chairs wear out, don't buy new ones. Simply buy new seats and backs which you can install yourself.

(9) Wrap packages at the post office. Many provide string, tape and (sometimes) address labels free.

(10) Before you buy anything—furniture, books, toys, jewelry, appliances—check at the Salvation Army, Good Will, garage sales, and salvage (freight-damaged) stores.

(11) Venetian blind repair shops collect barrels of sturdy, used cord. Ask for some and save yourself the expense of buying rope or string.

(12) Most ribbons attached to gifts come specially crafted as tight, reusable ribbons. Save them for gift-wrapping packages yourself.

(13) New or back-from-the-cleaners shirts, tablecloths, and other items often have straight pins (common pins) stuck several

places in them. Pluck out carefully and save to use as tacks for bulleting boards, basting pins, and other uses.

(14) Your morning paper probably comes in a small plastic bag or wrapped with a rubber band. Save the rubber bands and bags for later uses.

(15) Save old newspapers. Use to: (a) absorb grease when cooking, (b) stuff and cushion packages, (c) roll into "fireplace logs," (d) wrap frozen items to keep "cold" in, (e) spread over work areas, and (f) sell (price of old newspapers is increasing).

(16) The full width of a piece of "Scotch" tape rarely is needed. Tear or cut down the middle vertically. For example, if tape width is ¾", cut it down the middle and remaining strips of ⅜" will do most "sticking" jobs adequately.

(17) Photos through the mail as well as clothing, and dry cleaning items often come with separate sheets of cardboard backing. Save them for later use in packing or for poster boards.

(18) Save paper towel rolls to slip or tape over coat hangers to make them pants' hangers.

(19) Don't discard plastic raincoats badly torn. Repair kits for plastic swimming pools work as well with plastic raincoats.

(20) Use grocery sacks, butcher paper or layers of newspaper to cover books.

(21) Kids' school-rulers get lost easily. Drill hole and place in note book rings and they won't get lost.

(22) Keep empty pill bottles (plastic ones; glass ones can shatter and cut) to put paper clips in, bobby pins, loose change, kids' bank, etc.

(23) Don't buy a net for acquarium; make one from old nylon.

(24) Use laundry marking pencil or sew-on identification tags on kids' hats, coats, mittens, etc.

(25) Don't buy a baby scale. Weigh yourself, then weigh yourself with baby.

(26) Don't buy a bottle warmer. Remove percolator basket from coffee pot, fill up halfway with water, and use that.

(27) Save aluminum cans. Going rate is 15¢ per pound.

(28) Xeroxing charges (single page) vary from 5¢ to 20¢. Check around. Xerox machines in and around universities frequently have cheapest service.

(29) Many photos can be duplicated over Xerox machines. Use it and avoid expensive photo processing costs.

(30) Write Consumer Product Information, Wash., D.C.

20407. Ask for their catalog which lists roughly 220 booklets giving advice on specific consumer products. Some booklets are free; most range from 20¢ to $1.00.

NOTES

1. "How to Avoid Money Management Mistakes," bulletin of Financial Marketing Associates, 1972, p. 5.

2. Sidney Margoulis, *Family Money Problems*, Public Affairs Pamphlets, #142, p. 8.

3. "Facts and Fallacies on Food," *Houston Post*, March 7, 1974, p. 14A.

4. Tom Hall, "Night and Day in a Supermarket," *Catholic Digest*, October, 1974, pp. 102-110.

5. Cited in *Parade*, p. 7, January 1, 1975.

6. Lois McBride, "Feeding a Family of Four on $100 a Month," *Woman's Day*, August, 1972, p. 36.

7. "Food for Fitness," Consumer and Food Economics Research Division, Agricultural Research Service, Wash., D.C.

8. "Do We Eat Too Much Meat?" *Today's Health*, October, 1974, pp. 195, 197, 198.

9. Sidney Margoulis, *How to S-t-r-e-t-c-h Your Money*, Public Affairs Pamphlet.

10. "Now There's Meatless Meat," *Changing Times*, February, 1974, pp. 53, 54.

11. "1,000 'Farms' Planned on Lots in New York," Murray Schmach, *New York Times*, April 20, 1977, pp. 1 ff.

12. "Try Gardening in a Group," *Changing Times*, March, 1974, pp. 41 and 42 (Appleton, Wis.)

13. The *Victoria Advocate*, March 7, 1974, p. 46.

14. Courtesy Register and Tribune Syndicate, cited in *The Providence Journal*, September 4, 1975.

15. Source unknown.

16. *The Real Paper*, Boston, October 8, 1975, p. 3.

17. *Family Circle*, January, 1971, pp. 33, 87, 90.

18. "The Mother Earth News," *The Houston Post*, September 20, 1975, p. 4/AA.

19. Evelyn Kantor, "Sales and Bargains," *New York*, October 27, 1975, p. 95.

20. Courtesy King Features Syndicate, in *Providence Journal*, November 19, 1975, p. B-27.

21. Catherine Marshall, *To Live Again*, Avon Books, New York, 1975, pp. 81-84.

Appendix A

Fasting for Financial Relief and Famine Relief

Every recipe, budget tip, and savings recommendation given in this book has been based upon the premise that we are stewards of the riches God has entrusted to us.

Consider the stewardship involved in fasting:

On Mondays I don't eat (actually bedtime Sunday to noon Tuesday).

I began fasting two years ago. I do not know why I keep fasting, but it is a good discipline.

I'm addicted to food. Once I start eating, I don't want to stop. I'm told that a drug addict thinks only of the next fix; the alcoholic, of the next drink. When I eat, titillating my lips and warming my stomach, I am tempted to think not of work or service but of more food.

After supper: "More potatoes?"

"Yuh, okay, sweetie—and, uh, while you're in there put a little bit more gravy on it." (Well, I *have* to eat seconds; it makes my wife feel good.)

10:00 p.m.: "Want a bowl of ice cream?"

"Ah . . . okay . . . sounds like a winner."

(Well, *she'll* probably have a bowl and, you know, people don't like to eat alone.)

Along with the ice cream, I plunge my fist in a vanilla-wafer cookie box. (Can't eat ice cream by itself, you know.)

This is followed by an apple, a sandwich, a glass of milk, or something else I need "so that a sweet taste won't stay in the mouth."

It never fails. Once I start shoveling forkfuls of food and crunching snacks, I will not stop. I keep on shoveling and crunching, regardless of time, weight, or expense. And I always find excuses to deceive myself.

Fasting on Mondays has put a clamp on me. When I make my body say no to food on Mondays, it's a slap in the face lasting all week. I'm no longer driven to food. I'm in control of it, not vice versa.

The trauma of each Monday now is like someone shoving me in a chair, grabbing me by the shoulders, shaking me and shouting in my face, "Food is not important! When you start eating it tomorrow, remember, food is for fuel, not fun. When you start eating again, don't pack your stomach and intestines like you did yesterday after church." (Why do Sunday dinners absolve Christians from gluttony?)

Each Monday is like someone holding me under a freezing shower. I feel its bristle and shock all week. It awakens me to what is essential, and disciplines my daily life-style.

Fasting trims. I don't have a weight problem. And I don't intend to wait until I have one to say no to food. Fasting makes me acutely aware that my body is a divine building, a home for God's Spirit. It teaches me to be an alert manager of this body.

Reminding me of the responsibility to care for my body, fasting prompts me to exercise more—not just on Mondays, but all week. I run more, do more push-ups, sit-ups, and weight-lifting.

Fasting reminds me that it's foolish to wait until I'm middle-aged and obese before I decide to discipline my body. It reminds me that if I wait to exercise until I am middle-aged and heavy, I run the risk of putting too much strain on a forty-year-old, weak heart muscle. By staying thin through fasting and trim through exercising, I know I'll have little problem in exercising beyond middle-age years.

Fasting rearranges priorities. And eating is low on the scale of priorities. We eat primarily to get strength to do the important things. I know that now. I didn't before.

I used to arrange my schedule around: (1) breakfast, (2) coffee and doughnuts at 10, (3) lunch at 12, and (4) a big, heavy supper at 7:00 (used to spend more time eating at night than reading to the kids). Very subtly, almost unconsciously, I arranged my schedule to meet someone at lunchtime who'd probably suggest lunching while talking (didn't matter if he paid for it or I, as long as I got the chance to eat). I arranged to visit people at home not always on the basis of their needs, but on the basis of who'd most likely feed me cake and coffee.

My schedule revolved around food. As a matter of fact, the entire American schedule revolves around food.

Up. Breakfast . . . dum, dum, dum, dum, dum. . . . Coffee and snack . . . dum, dum, dum, dum, dum. . . . Lunch . . . dum, dum, dum, dum, dum. . . . Coffee and snack . . . dum, dum, dum, dum, dum. . . . Supper . . . dum, dum, dum, dum, dum. . . . TV snack or midnight snack.

Food is a priority item with us. We spend more, *much more* time and money on it than it's worth. Madison Avenue and the food industry want it that way and we usually go along. Tom Hall's comment is worth a second look:

> If they really wanted the ultimate in good nutrition and price, then the food industry would devise some cheap, effortless, and excellent nutrient like dog food. People would just reach into a paper sack and grab a handful and eat it. Nobody would be fat or have high blood pressure. Kitchens would become closets. Supermarkets would become filling stations. The average middle class American would be 10% richer, having saved most of the 15.7% of his income that he now spends on food. And he would have two hours more each day to do what he likes, having reduced his mealtimes to a grab and swallow. ("Night and Day in a Supermarket," *Catholic Digest*, October, 1974, pp. 102-110.)

Fasting on Mondays keeps reminding me that I need only to go to the filling station periodically during the week. Fasting reminds me that food is for fuel to keep going, not for fun.

Since fasting, I have more money to send to famine peoples. I estimate that by not eating on Monday, I save at least two dollars, which I'm then able to send to a famine-fighting organization (usually World Vision, 919 W. Huntington Drive, Monrovia, California).

And, since fasting restricts not only excess food but *substance* food, I'm learning anew each week that the world's hungry will really be fed only when the rich (us) are willing to give from our substance, not excess.

Fasting reminds me of hunger and provokes me to count my blessings. It's been a long time since I've felt involuntary hunger. As a boy, off and on welfare, holed up in freezing tenements during New England winters, I remember shuffling to school hungry. I remember going to a school cafeteria hungry and smelling molasses-coated baked beans, steaming-hot buttered rolls, and butterscotch-brown cookies. I remember sitting alone at a table, head aching and staring into a book, pretending I was so absorbed in reading that I didn't care about eating. I remember shuffling home again, hungry.

I went to college and got rich. Teaching in the Peace Corps, I made $75 a month, and ate three meals a day. That was ten years ago, and I've been eating three meals a day every since (or can, if I want to). I forget what hunger is. On Mondays I remember.

Fasting has disarmed Satan; it has lessened the spheres of his attacks on me. Constant eating—meal after meal, day after day, week after week—depletes my energies, weakens my discipline, injures my intimacy with God, and opens up avenues of attack for Satan. Relentless eating eventually makes my flesh and spirit just as flabby as would relentless drugs or beer. Twenty-one meals a week (for me) is relentless eating. It hardly disciplines my body for work and service. Fasting on Mondays is a punch in Satan's face, driving him away from this body.

Understand, please, that there are extremes of fasting. Fasting does not mean one denies food and its proper enjoyment. As a matter of fact, I enjoy food *more* now since I'm in control of it and not vice versa. My wife bakes Mexican enchiladas dripping with yellow cheese and red pepper sauce, onion rolls, soft, hot, and tangy, and the best deep-dish, sausage-layered lasagne this side of Milan. I love them all and want to enjoy them, not be controlled by them.

Another extreme in this business of fasting is to force it on people. Whenever priests, preachers, deacons or elders dictate a decision that on such-or-such a day or month everyone will fast, they're out of line.* Fasting is voluntary, between man and God only.

Another extreme is dictating *how* to do it. I fast from Sunday night to Tuesday noon, usually with water and sometimes juice. Sometimes I go longer than Tuesday noon. I know dedicated Christians who fast for ten days, drinking liquids only. I know equally dedicated Christians able to fast from bedtime to noon

---

*I do not think that events like a National Day for Prayer and Fasting constitute dictated decisions. They are *invitations* to fast for a collective purpose, totally appropriate.

the next day only. Everyone's metabolism is different. No one can impose his fasting schedule on another. How one fasts is between man and God only.

Another extreme is to "crash" into fasting. Don't do it. Plan it, pray for it, and check with a doctor before extended fasting.

Another extreme is not fasting at all.

Appendix B

Understanding Biblical Principles and Personal Finances

Accounting

"So then every one of us shall give account of himself to God" (Rom. 14:12).

"Therefore is the kingdom of heaven likened unto a certain king, which would take account of his servants" (Matt. 18:23).

Parable of the Talents (Matt. 25:14-30).

Prosperity

"And he shall be like a tree planted by the rivers of water, that bringeth forth his fruit in his season; his leaf also shall not wither; and whatsoever he doeth shall prosper" (Ps. 1:3).

"He is like a tree planted by water, that sends out its roots by the stream, and does not fear when heat comes, for its leaves remain green, and is not anxious in the year of drought, for it does not cease to bear fruit. The heart is deceitful above all things, and desperately corrupt; who can understand it?" (Jer. 17:8, 9, RSV).

"And his master saw that the Lord was with him, and that the Lord made all that he did to prosper in his hand" (Gen. 39:3).

"For ye know the grace of our Lord Jesus Christ, that, though he was rich, yet for your sakes he became poor, that ye through his poverty might be rich" (2 Cor. 8:9).

"Beloved, I wish above all things that thou mayest prosper and be in health, even as thy soul prospereth" (3 John 2).

"Be strong and of a good courage: for unto this people shalt thou divide for an inheritance the land, which I sware unto their fathers to give them. Only be thou strong and very courageous, that thou mayest observe to do according to all the law, which Moses my servant commanded thee: turn not from it to the right hand or to the left, that thou mayest prosper withersoever thou goest. This book of the law shall not depart out of thy mouth; but thou shalt meditate therein day and night, that thou mayest observe to do according to all that is written therein: for then thou shalt make thy way prosperous, and then thou shalt have good success success" (Joshua 1:6-8).

Debt

"Owe no man anything, but to love one another" (Rom. 13:8).

"He will bless you as he has promised. You shall lend money to many nations but will never need to borrow! You shall rule many nations, but they shall not rule over you!" (Deut. 15:6, LB).

"Just as the rich rule the poor, so the borrower is servant to the lender" (Prov. 22:7, LB).

"One day the wife of one of the seminary students came to Elisha to tell him of her husband's death. He was a man who had loved God, she said. But he had owed some money when he died, and now the creditor was demanding it back. If she didn't pay, he said he would take her two sons as his slaves" (2 Kings 4:1, LB).

Tithing and Giving

"Bring ye all the tithes into the storehouse, that there may be meat in mine house, and prove me now herewith, saith the Lord of hosts, if I will not open you the windows of heaven, and pour you out a blessing, that there shall not be room enough to receive it" (Mal. 3:10).

"Bring this tithe to eat before the Lord your God at the place he shall choose as his sanctuary; this applies to your tithes of grain, new wine, olive oil, and the first-born of your flocks and herds. The purpose of tithing is to teach you always to put God first in your lives" (Deut. 14:23, LB).

"Honor the Lord by giving him the first part of all your income, and he will fill your barns with wheat and barley and overflow your wine vats with the finest wines" (Prov. 3:9, 10, LB).

"Yes, woe upon you, Pharisees, and you other religious leaders—hypocrites! For you tithe down to the last mint leaf in your garden, but ignore the important things—justice and mercy and faith. Yes, you should tithe, but you shouldn't leave the more important things undone" (Matt. 23:23, LB).

"Upon the first day of the week let every one of you lay by him in store, as God hath prospered him, that there be no gatherings when I come" (1 Cor. 16:2).

"But remember this—if you give little, you will get little. A farmer who plants just a few seeds will get only a small crop, but if he plants much, he will reap much. Everyone must make up his own mind as to how much he should give. Don't force anyone to give more than he really wants to, for cheerful givers are the ones God prizes. God is able to make it up to you by giving you everything you need and more, so that there will not only be enough for your own needs, but plenty left over to give joyfully to others" (2 Cor. 9:6-8, LB).

"This Melchizedek was king of the city of Salem, and also a priest of the Most High God. When Abraham was returning home after winning a great battle against many kings, Malchizedek met him and blessed him; then Abraham took a tenth of all he had won in the battle and gave it to Melchizedek" (Heb. 7:1, 2, LB).

Where Is His Wealth?

"For God giveth to a man that is good in his sight wisdom, and knowledge, and joy: but to the sinner he giveth travail, to gather and to heap up, that he may give to him that is good before God. This also is vanity and vexation of spirit" (Eccles. 2:26).

"Obey the laws of the Lord your God. Walk in his ways and fear him. For the Lord your God is bringing you into a good land of brooks, pools, gushing springs, valleys, and hills; it is a land of wheat and barley, of grape vines, fig trees, pomegranates, olives, and honey; it is a land where food is plentiful and nothing is lacking; it is a land where iron is as common as stone, and copper is abundant as the hills" (Deut. 8:6-9, LB).

"For every beast of the forest is mine, and the cattle upon a thousand hills. I know all the fowls of the mountains: and the wild beasts of the field are mine. If I were hungry, I would not tell thee: for the world is mine and the fulness thereof" (Ps. 50:10-12).

What Are Needs?

"Therefore I tell you, do not be anxious about your life, what you shall eat or what you shall drink, nor about your body, what you shall put on. Is not life more than food, and the body more than clothing? Look at the birds of the air: they neither sow nor reap nor gather into barns, and yet your heavenly Father feeds them. Are you not of more value than they? And which of you by being anxious can add one cubit to his span of life? And why are you anxious about clothing? Consider the lilies of the field, how they grow; they neither toil nor spin; yet I tell you, even Solomon in all his glory was not arrayed like one of these. But if God so clothes the grass of the field, which today is alive and tomorrow is thrown into the oven, will he not much more clothe you, O men of little faith? Therefore do not be anxious, saying, 'What shall we eat?' or 'What shall we drink?' or 'What shall we wear?' For the Gentiles seek all these things; and your heavenly Father knows that you need them all. But seek first his kingdom and his righteousness, and all these things shall be yours as well" (Matt. 6:25-33, RSV).

Planning

"For which of you, intending to build a tower, sitteth not down first, and counteth the cost, whether he have sufficient to finish it? Lest haply, after he hath laid the foundation, and is not able to finish it, all that behold it begin to mock him, saying, This man began to build, and was not able to finish" (Luke 14:28-30).

Parable of the Rich Fool (Luke 12:16-21).

Parable of the Unjust Steward (Luke 16:1-8).

"Now concerning the collection of the saints, as I have given order to the churches of Galatia, even so do ye. Upon the first day of the week let every one of you lay by him in store, as God hath prospered him, that there be no gatherings when I come" (1 Cor. 16:1, 2).

"For God so loved the world, that he gave his only begotten Son, that whosoever believeth in him should not perish but have everlasting life" (John 3:16).

Examples of Planning

Joseph (Gen. 37-41).
(We are the corporate Joseph.)

Character of God's Steward—Joseph

Forgiveness, compassion, love, desire to live as a righteous man, desire to serve.

God's Provision

Genesis 41—Provision was through a PLAN.
Exodus 15—Moses.
1 Kings 17—Elijah.
2 Kings 4—Elisha.
John 21:2—Peter.
Matthew 4:11—Jesus.
Luke 12:7—His people.

Business Life

Honesty vs. Unjust Gain

"Recompense to no man evil for evil. Provide things honest in the sight of all men" (Rom. 12:17).

"A false balance is abomination to the Lord: but a just weight is his delight" (Prov. 11:1).

"But thou shalt have a perfect and just weight, a perfect and just measure shalt thou have: that thy days may be lengthened in the land which the Lord thy God giveth thee" (Deut. 25:15).

"Better is a little with righteousness, than great revenues without right" (Prov. 16:8).

"He that oppresseth the poor to increase his riches, and he that giveth to the rich, shall surely come to want" (Prov. 22:16).

"Income from exploiting the poor will end up in the hands of someone who pities them" (Prov. 28:8, LB).

"Woe to him . . . that useth his neighbor's service without wages, and giveth him not for his work" (Jer. 22:13).

"He that is faithful in that which is least is faithful also in much; and he that is unjust in the least is unjust also in much" (Luke 16:10).

Attitudes and Actions

"The soul of the sluggard desireth, and hath nothing: but the soul of the diligent shall be made fat" (Prov. 13:4).

"He becometh poor that dealeth with a slack hand: but the

hand of the diligent maketh rich" (Prov. 10:4).

"Wealth gotten by vanity shall be diminished: but he that gathereth by labour shall increase" (Prov. 13:11).

"Not slothful in business; fervent in spirit; serving the Lord" (Rom. 12:11).

"You shall not rob nor oppress anyone and you shall pay your hired workers promptly" (Lev. 19:13, LB).

God's action. "And I will come near to you to judgment; . . . against those that oppress the hireling in his wages" (Mal. 3:5).

"A good man sheweth favour, and lendeth: he will guide his affairs with discretion" (Ps. 112:5).

"But love ye your enemies, and do good, and lend, hoping for nothing again; and your reward shall be great" (Luke 6:35a).

"The sleep of a labouring man is sweet, whether he eat little or much: but the abundance of the rich will not suffer him to sleep" (Eccles. 5:12).

" . . . rather let him labour, working with his hands the thing which is good, that he may have to give to him that needeth" (Eph. 4:28).

"You are a poor specimen if you can't stand the pressure of adversity" (Prov. 24:10, LB).

Jesus spoke of planning and counting the cost before we build (Luke 14:28-39). A budget is a plan.

"A wise man thinks ahead; a fool doesn't, and even brags about it" (Prov. 13:16, LB).

"We can make our plans, but the final outcome is in God's hands" (Prov. 16:1, LB).

"We should make plans—counting on God to direct us" (Prov. 16:9, LB).

"The wise man saves for the future, but the foolish man spends whatever he gets" (Prov. 21:20, LB).

"A prudent man forsees the difficulties ahead and prepares for them; the simpleton goes blindly on and suffers the consequences" (Prov. 22:3, LB).

"A sensible man watches for problems ahead and prepares to meet them. The simpleton never looks, and suffers the consequences" (Prov. 27:12, LB).

"He who loves money will never have enough. The foolishness of thinking that wealth brings happiness. The more you have, the more you spend, right up to the limits of your income. So what is the advantage of wealth—except perhaps to watch it as it runs through your fingers" (Eccles. 5:10, 11).

Appendix C

Sample Budgets

Monthly Fixed Expenses

Church giving	
Home mortgage	
Home insurance	
Home taxes	
Emergency and savings	
Life insurance	
Health: accident: hospitalization	
Car insurance	
Other insurance: school, camper, boat, summer home	
Other taxes: excise, poll, land, personal property	
Other: union, club or other dues	
Total fixed expenses	

Monthly Flexible Expenses

Food	
Clothing	
Gas	
Water	
Electricity	
Heating	
Telephone	
Home improvements	
Home furnishings	
Home maintenance	
Contributions: United Way, Boy/Girl Scouts; Red Cross, etc.	
Car: repair, maintenance, gas and oil, registration, license	
Medical and dental	
Drugs	
Subscriptions: professional, regular, papers, books, tapes	
School: lunches, supplies, lunches at work, coffee breaks	
Cleaning, laundry	
Allowances	

Toiletries, cosmetics	
Stationery supplies, stamps, etc.	
Recreation, dinners, vacations, baby-sitters, bowling, etc.	
Dancing, music, tutoring	
Gifts: Christmas, anniversary, birthday, etc.	
Other:	
Total flexible expenses	
Total monthly expenses	
Total installment loan payments	
TOTAL MONTHLY EXPENDITURES	
Net monthly spendable income	
BALANCE—overage or shortage	

Month Of _____

Budget Worksheet—Page One

Date	Income	Church	Home Mortgage	Home Ins.	Home Taxes	Emerg. & Savings	Life Ins.	Health & Acc.	Car Ins.	Other Ins.	Food	Clothes	Gas	Water	Elec.	Total

Budget Worksheet—Page Two

Date	Heat	Home	Other Gifts	Car	Medical & Drugs	Subscrip.	School	Cleaning	Allow- ances	Personal	Recre- tion	Family Gifts	Other	Phone	Total Page 1	Total